Praise for *One God, Many Paths: Finding Meaning and Inspiration in Jewish Teachings*

MW00912730

"Amy Lederman is honest, funny, personal, and inspiring. To read her writing is to feel in the company of a beloved friend. *One God, Many Paths* grounds us in the Jewish tradition and universal life experience and elevates us to be our best."

> Rabbi Elie Kaplan Spitz, author of *Does the Soul Survive? A Jewish Journey to Belief in Afterlife, Past Lives & Living with Purpose* and *Healing from Despair: Choosing Wholeness in a Broken World*

"Amy Hirshberg Lederman's *One God, Many Paths* is a warm and accessible account of the ways that the teachings of Judaism can illuminate the day-to-day events of our lives. These short reflections are presented with deep affection, humor, and a wise and steady focus on the things that really matter to all of us."

> Dr. Barry W. Holtz, professor of Jewish Education at the Jewish Theological Seminary of America and author of *Back to the Sources: Reading the Classic Jewish Texts* and *Finding Our Way: Jewish Texts and the Lives We Lead Today*

"This is a sage, moving and imminently practical guide to living a life of meaning. Amy is a gifted teacher who writes with a spirit voice. I love this book and know you will too!"

> Eve A. Wood, MD, author of *There's Always Help; There's Always Hope* and *10 Steps to Take Charge of Your Emotional Life*

"Amy Hirshberg Lederman's *One God, Many Paths* strikes the perfect balance between spirituality and everyday life. Her practical wisdom—backed up by humor, honesty and a fresh perspective on religious ideals—makes *One God, Many Paths* the book for anyone searching for a better, more authentic way to live."

> Robin Brande, author of *Evolution, Me, and Other Freaks of Nature*

"Warm, inviting, and real, you will enjoy the Jewish journeys in this book. From the first page, Amy confides candidly, as she shares her feelings, questions and discoveries from the treasures of Jewish texts. Her gentle style will give you the sense that you are talking with a close friend, sitting next to you on the couch."

> Gil Mann, author of *How to Get More out of Being Jewish, Even If…* (www.beingjewish.org)

"Amy Lederman is a modern parabalist, who whose thoughtful and wise teachings of the Jewish tradition become a pathway to the sacred. Through the prism of her insight, the ordinary becomes extraordinary, and the everyday becomes holy. *One God, Many Paths* is a book for everyone who strives for a life of meaning and worth, goodness and right."

> Rabbi Wayne Dosick, PhD, author of *Living Judaism*, *Soul Judaism*, and *20 Minute Kabbalah*.

"*One God, Many Paths* contains moving examples of how wrestling with Jewish tradition can bring meaning into your life."

> Rabbi Laura Geller, senior rabbi, Temple Emanuel of Beverly Hills

ONE GOD, MANY PATHS

Finding Meaning and Inspiration in Jewish Teachings

Amy Hirshberg Lederman

One God, Many Paths: Finding Meaning and Inspiration in Jewish Teachings

For more information about the author, visit
www.amyhirshberglederman.com

Front cover artwork: Gail T. Roberts
Author photograph: Marcia Gold
Copyediting: Kaye Patchett
Book title inspiration: Bobbi Paley

Published by Wheatmark®
610 East Delano Street, Suite 104
Tucson, Arizona 85705 U.S.A.
www.wheatmark.com

International Standard Book Number: 978-1-58736-736-6
Library of Congress Control Number: 2007940700

I dedicate this book in love and appreciation…

To my teachers, who have inspired and challenged me,
To my students, who have taught me so much,
To my friends, who have encouraged and loved me along the way,
To my family, who has given me so much to write about!
To my husband, who has nurtured my very best,
To God, from whom all blessings flow,

I am forever grateful.

"I am a creature of God and my neighbor is also a creature of God.

I work in the city and he works in the country.

I rise early for my work and he rises early for his work.

Just as he cannot excel in my work, I cannot excel in his work.

Will you say that I do great things and he does small things?

We have learned that it does not matter whether a person does much or little, as long as he directs his heart to heaven."

Babylonian Talmud
Berakhot 17a

Contents

Learning through Living

Living with Integrity

Questioning As an Act of Faith

Celebrating the Joys, Not the Oys!

A Note to My Readers

I have a confession to make. I am in love—seriously, passionately and unabashedly. Not just with my husband of 25 years, but with a culture, faith, and community that has enriched my life beyond measure. Yes, I am in love with being Jewish because, to borrow a line from Jack Nicholson in *As Good as it Gets,* "It makes me want to be a better person."

But I did not always feel this way. For many years I secretly harbored a fear that I was somehow Jewishly deficient, maybe even a "bad" Jew, because I was not brought up in a home with Jewish traditions and rituals. Like many first generation Americans, my parents were good people who understood culturally what it meant to be Jewish but had little interest in maintaining Judaism at home. So while they sent me to Hebrew school, and taught me Jewish values like the importance of family and education, I never lit candles on Friday night or knew the first thing about keeping kosher.

The older I got, the more embarrassed I was to admit that I didn't know half of what I thought a "good" Jewish adult should know. But I had the good fortune of finding wonderful teachers along the way who encouraged me to ask questions and seek answers from Judaism, without shame or regret. I became addicted to questioning and the more I learned, the more I wanted to know. What I didn't realize at the time was how very Jewish my approach was—that questioning for the purpose of true understanding is an act of faith in itself.

And this is what I learned: that Judaism is an action-oriented faith that elevates what we do (deed) over what we believe (creed). We have been given a marvelous blueprint for living called the Torah which contains 613 commandments to help us choose wisely in all aspects of our life. Some believe that the Torah is the Divine Revelation of God; others believe it is the inspired authorship of man. In either case, at the heart of the Torah is the central idea that everything we do and say has the potential for holiness. It is up to us to make the choice, each day of our lives, as to how we want to live.

I wrote *One God, Many Paths: Finding Meaning and Inspiration in Jewish Teachings* because I wanted to share my passion for Jewish wisdom with others who are curious, interested or may not be aware of the richness and relevancy that can be found in the treasury of sacred Jewish texts. It is my hope that anyone who reads these stories, regardless of age, religious background or degree of observance, will be inspired by the wisdom of the ages and sages, uplifted by the messages of hope and resilience and encouraged to explore the meaning that these texts may have in their life, family and world.

The
Search for
Meaning

Lech Lecha: *The Jewish Search for Meaning and Purpose*

I f I got paid for the amount of time I spend looking for my car keys or cell phone, I could quit my day job. My husband is no better. He passes me in the hall, sleuth-like and squinting, searching for his glasses or wallet. Inevitably, he calls out in exasperation from the bedroom. "Where did YOU put my wallet?"

"I hid it in your pants pocket, the ones that are still in the dryer," I call out gaily as I locate my cell phone under the newspaper.

On a serious note, most of us spend a great deal of our lives searching—for love, meaning, identity and purpose. In our youth, we seek parental approval, friendship, social acceptance and new experiences. As young adults, we look for loving relationships, a quality education and career, freedom of expression, perhaps our first home. And for many years thereafter, we continue the search— for the right partner, the best opportunities for our kids, meaningful friendships, spiritual fulfillment and communities in which we feel accepted and appreciated.

As different as we are from one another, the human need to find and make meaning from our life is a common bond between us. Whether this need stems from the ego, our inner voice or Divine Guidance, the search for identity, belonging, and self-worth is what drives us to develop ourselves and reach our highest potential.

The questions that impel our search for meaning often sound like this: "What is the meaning of my life? Do I have a purpose? Am I on the right path? Am I making a difference?" But the answers to these questions often come in the form of fears like this: "Am I good enough/talented enough/smart enough? What if I fail? What will others think of me? Whom will I disappoint if I change?"

The quintessential "search story" in Judaism is found in the Torah. It begins with one person, Abraham, who was called upon by God to journey with his wife to a foreign land. God told Abraham: "*Lech Lecha*! Go for yourself from your land, from your relatives, and from your father's house to the land that I will show you. And I will make of you a great nation; and I will bless you and make your name great and you shall be a blessing."

Abraham was asked to give up everything he knew, to sever all ties with his family, friends, community and home, to follow God's lead. Looking at this story with contemporary eyes, I am amazed at Abraham's courage and *chutzpah*. Here was a man living in a world ruled by multiple gods and superstitions who followed a voice that no one else could fathom, let alone hear. By our standards it seems, I don't know… crazy? Undoubtedly many thought so at the time. Dangerous? Most certainly, as Abraham encountered enemies, famine and war on his journey to Canaan. Inspiring? Most definitely, if we let the message of Lech Lecha become a directive for us in our lives today.

God's instruction to Abraham to leave his past was enhanced by the promise that Abraham's future would include children; in fact, multitudes of descendants. This was no small thing considering that his wife Sarah, at the age of 65, had not yet conceived. He was also told he would become great, a standard by which others would measure and bless themselves. Simply put, Abraham was given a Divine purpose that helped him understand the significance of the journey he was about to undertake.

Abraham was able to follow his heart because of two important reasons: he had faith and he had trust. Faith in the Divine guidance he received, which enabled him alone to hear and understand the purpose of his life. And trust, that no matter how difficult or dangerous the journey might be, it would be worth it because he would become the man he was destined to become.

The story of Lech Lecha beckons us, as humans and as Jews, to take risks and travel into the unknown in pursuit of our true purpose or purposes in life. It encourages us to listen to our intuitions, to pay attention to the inner voice that more often directs our heart than our head. It teaches us that we may have to leave what we know and move away from areas of comfort, stability and ease, in order to develop our potential and become our most authentic selves. Like Abraham, we may appear crazy for leaving a job that seems perfect or a lifestyle that others covet. But like Abraham, if we hear the call, we must remember to put our faith in that inner voice that guides us along the way, whatever or however we define it, and trust in our strength, ability, creativity and talents that if we make the journey, we too, may find our own "promised land."

Life at 40: Divine Intervention or Mere Coincidence?

The number 40 in the Jewish tradition holds a unique spot in our history and our psyche. The flood during Noah's time lasted for 40 days. Moses went up to the mountain to receive the Torah and spoke with God for 40 days and 40 nights. The Hebrew people wandered in the desert for 40 years prior to reaching the land of Israel. The legal status of an embryo changes from "fluid" to "potential life" after the fortieth day. We are forbidden to study the Kabbalah or engage in Jewish metaphysics until we have reached the age of 40.

I am not a superstitious person. In fact, I am down-right skeptical about things like palm readers, tarot cards and Ouija boards. Yet I can't help but think that it was more than just coincidence that my own life-altering experience occurred during the month that I celebrated my fortieth birthday.

It had been a banner year for me. My law practice was booming, my two young children were thriving, and my husband and I celebrated our tenth anniversary—still very much in love. "If only I could stop the clock right now," I thought, recalling the many times I had heard my father say those words to me when I was little.

Then I got sick; I mean really sick. Things escalated from bad to worse as I lay delirious in bed, my fever inching above 105. It didn't help that it was New Year's weekend, when even the most dedicated med-school resident was nowhere to be found. I don't remember much about that time, thankfully, except for the memory of my family hovering over me and my children asking my husband if I would die. It took several days of my husband's persistence until we finally realized that I was having an allergic reaction to an antibiotic that I was taking. Weeks of steroids later, I re-entered life with a puffy face and a renewed awareness of how precious each day truly is.

What happened during those few bleak days, however, is what I have come to view as my own personal wake-up call from God. Because during that time something happened inside of me and I soon realized that, like it or not, there was no going back. Four months later, while I was eating breakfast with my husband, I told him about my epiphany.

"I'm thinking of closing my law practice to study Judaism," I said as I stirred milk into my coffee.

"And I'm thinking of growing my hair out and becoming a rock star," he crooned.

"No, I mean it. I had this revelation when I was sick. I realized that I don't want to wake up on the other side of 50 without having taken the risk of going after what I truly believe I am meant to do. I want to study, learn and teach Judaism."

Several hundred conversations later, I embarked on a journey that has changed my life for the better in ways too numerous to count. I worked hard, studied hard and learned from some of the finest teachers from Tucson to Jerusalem. I had no idea when I began this journey 13 years ago where it would lead, but I had faith that whatever the outcome, I would be a better person for having made the effort.

I look back on what happened in my fortieth year as more than mere coincidence. There was a reason I got sick, although I certainly didn't understand it at the time. Whether it happened because of an infection, a faulty medical diagnosis or Divine intervention, it opened the doors of my heart to help me understand something important about my life.

Each of us will encounter difficulties in our lifetime, from financial struggles and failed relationships to personal tragedies and crises of faith. But it is how we respond to what happens to us that determines who we become as we live out our lives. We alone can decide if we will let our experiences become catalysts for personal growth or stumbling blocks to our development. The true mystery lies in whether we will be able to hear that inner voice when it speaks to us about our life and the choices we have made. And when we do hear it, whether we will have the courage to follow it when it requires us to change.

Jewish tradition teaches that although everything is anticipated by God, each one of us is the author of our own actions, accountable for our choices. Sometimes it is hard to explain—to ourselves and to others—why we act the way we do. But in moments of personal enlightenment, a spark of the Divine can be seen. The Talmudic rabbis said it beautifully when they wrote: "All is foreseen, but freedom of choice is given; and the world is judged with goodness, and all is in accordance with the works."

(Pirkei Avot 3:15)

Is Being Good, Good Enough?

I boarded the plane, my briefcase overflowing with the books I wanted to read during the five hour flight: A novel about Afghanistan, a *Rolling Stone Magazine* I found in my daughter's bathroom and a book on Jewish ethics. I opened up the ethics book and began scribbling notes in the margin as I read. The woman next to me maneuvered her body in order to read the summary on the book jacket as I continued to write.

"I'm a Jew but I'm not religious," she announced somewhat defensively. "I stopped going to Temple after my kids grew up and I don't keep the Sabbath like my parents did. But I make a great honey cake and belong to Haddassah," she concluded defiantly.

Oh great, I thought, keeping my eyes on the page. All I want to do is eat my little bag of honey-roasted peanuts and read my book in peace. Now I'm going to have to listen to this woman's entire life story.

I nodded my head in silence, but did not look up. Then the irony of the situation hit me like a brick—especially in light of the paragraph I had just finished reading. The image was fresh in my mind: that humans are God's most exceptional "works of art" and that from the moment of birth, we are given continuous opportunities to turn our lives into masterpieces. We fashion our lives using the tools found in the Torah, the primary one being Jewish ethics—how we relate to, honor and treat others, including God, as we live out each day.

I felt a bit sheepish as I looked into the woman's face. I couldn't ignore the obvious: that my avoidance bordered on rudeness.

What is it about being a "good person" that has such a hold on me? Am I afraid that if I'm not nice enough or good enough, people will think I'm unethical? What are ethics anyway? Are they values that make us feel good when we do them, like being nice to a stranger, but guilty when we don't? Are they absolute laws like the Ten Commandments? Are they universal or personal, absolute or conditional, pragmatic or hypothetical? Are they God-given or man-made?

Jewish living is governed by Jewish law or *Halakah*, which in Hebrew literally means "the path that one walks." Halakah is made up of the 613 Commandments (*Mitzvot*) from the Torah and deals with all categories of life—from ritual practices to business ethics, from appropriate dress to family relationships, from acts of charity to proper sexual conduct. There is no distinction in the Torah between what is religious and what is secular. Simply put, everything we do has the potential for holiness.

In the very center of the Torah is a Chapter called the Holiness Code, which tells us what is expected of us as human beings: "You shall be holy, for I, the Lord your God, am holy." We learn two significant things from this passage: First, that God is holy, and second, that God expects us to be holy. We are given the Torah and all of its laws as a blueprint for living a good life, a holy life. We are taught that we can become holy, and therefore more God-like, when we sanctify and honor special times, places, events and relationships. In our struggle to be good people, we are given a roadmap to guide us toward becoming the most complete human masterpieces that we can become.

The flight attendant announced that we could move about the cabin if we wanted. I put my book mark in the place where I had stopped reading and the words of Rabbi Nachman of Bratslav jumped off the page: "In seeking to sanctify God's Name, each person has something in life which is more a barrier than anything else. This is precisely the barrier we have to overcome in order to serve God."

My seat-mate hadn't stopped talking since take-off, but I felt differently now. For in the past half-hour, she had become real to me and I realized that we weren't very different after all. We were just two Jewish women flying side by side, trying our best to muddle through life and become better people and ultimately better Jews.

Charitable Donations:
Why Should I Give?

I opened my mailbox to find several letters, a few bills and a host of requests for donations from various organizations that I have supported over the years. Because I am a stickler for organization, I sort the letters, place the bills in a folder marked "Look at me soon!" and the appeals for donations in one marked "Save the World." Between the needs of my local community, the Jewish community, our country and the world at large, I am seriously thinking about renting a storage unit for the hundreds of solicitations that I receive annually.

I don't know how you think about charitable giving, but I am honestly confused about it myself. Year after year, questions continue to gnaw at me: What is the right amount for a gift? Should I support Jewish organizations first and then donate to other charities only after I have made my Jewish gifts? Why am I giving in the first place? Does it need to "hurt" for my gift to be meaningful? Am I willing to give up something—a dinner out, theater tickets, a trip—to make a more substantial contribution this year?

Tzedakah, the Jewish commandment to give, has

been a quintessential Jewish value since the beginning of Jewish time. The Torah teaches that "If there is a needy person among you, any of your brethren in any of your cities in the Land that God has given you, you shall not harden your heart or close your hand against him. Rather, you shall open your hand and lend him whatever he is lacking." (Deut. 15:7-8)

Tzedakah is the counterpart to *Tikkun Olam*, the Jewish obligation to repair the world. Both affirm our responsibility to distribute a part of what we have to take care of others who are less fortunate. Both are grounded in the idea that individual wealth is neither a right nor a privilege but a form of stewardship for which we are charged, as agents of God, to care for the world in which we live.

These obligations operate in concentric circles— originating within our own home and family, extending out into the Jewish community and then to the world. Jewish law specifically recognizes that *any* needy person who lives in peaceful coexistence with us is a worthy charitable recipient. The Talmud teaches that we should help support the poor even outside our own community, because of the "ways of peace." (Gittin 59 b)

Jewish law is fairly specific in its answer to the question of what we should give. Ideally, we are expected to give what is needed to help restore a poor person to his or her former position. If a man has lost all of his clothing in a fire, we should help him purchase clothes. If he has lost his job, we should provide him with employment either directly or indirectly by helping him find work. The

Jewish sage Maimonides established specific parameters
for giving with the average acceptable gift as 10 percent
of our possessions and the ideal gift as 20 percent. But
Jewish law is both practical and realistic in its demands
because it never requires us to become lacking or poor
ourselves as a result of giving.

The critical question we each need to answer is: Why
do I give? What makes me want to give? Is it because
of peer or professional pressure, social recognition or a
genuine commitment to the cause?

I am inspired by the words of Moses when he told
the Israelites to bring gifts to build the Tabernacle, saying:
"Take from among you gifts to the Lord: everyone *whose
heart so moves him* shall bring them…." (Ex. 35:5) When
we give, Jewish tradition asks that we open rather than
harden our hearts—because it is from our hearts, not
our heads, that we are more inclined to see the needs of
others and give willingly, meaningfully and generously.

During our lives we will have times when our resources
and income may be limited. Some of us will struggle
more than others. An unexpected tragedy or illness can
make it nearly impossible to give. But Tzedakah is an
"equal opportunity mitzvah" and applies to everyone, no
matter how great or small our portion. If we are unable
to give of our money, we can give of our time, talents
and wisdom. Our sages assured us that we are all capable
of giving, even one who receives tzedakah, when they
said: "To the one who is eager to give, God provides the
means."

Don't Sweat the Small Stuff...
or Should You?

My friend Susan is a stickler for niceties. She sends thank you cards within days of receiving a gift, responds to an invitation before the R.S.V.P. due date, and puts the shopping cart back at the grocery store. And if she is late, she always calls to give a minute-by-minute update of when she will arrive.

Watching Susan has made me realize that many of the courtesies that were commonplace in the past have all but disappeared from contemporary life. Susan has a theory about this. She thinks that we have become a society that equates being busy with being important; that the busier we are, the more important we think we are. So we have stopped doing some of the smaller, less important things, like saying thank you to a cashier or letting a car merge in front of us in traffic, because we no longer have time to fit them into our overly-busy, super-important lives.

Susan doesn't consider herself a "religious" person. She doesn't attend synagogue regularly and when her daughter didn't want to have a Bat Mitzvah, she didn't force the issue. Yet while she is attending to what may look like the "minutiae of life," she is also honoring a very Jewish concept—that the way we speak, act and respond to others in our daily life is a reflection of the way we honor each other, and ultimately, honor God.

Jewish tradition teaches us that we are created *B'Tzelem Elohim*, which means "in the likeness or image of God." (Genesis 1:27) In our struggle to live a good and meaningful life, being created in the image of God can help guide our choices and direct our actions. It sets a standard as we develop and define our potential, capabilities and relationships. More importantly, when we act with an awareness that every single one of us is created in God's image, we elevate not only ourselves but others with whom we interact.

Imagine this scenario: You are in line at the grocery store and the cashier is wearing a T-shirt with the words: "Handle with Care. Created in the Image of God." How would you react? Would you pause before paying your bill, perhaps to smile or acknowledge her?

What if you were in a tense meeting at work, negotiating with your competitor, or arguing with your colleague who was wearing a similar T-shirt? Would you be less inclined to interrupt? Would you try harder to understand his point of view?

These examples might seem a bit of a stretch but the point is that we might act differently toward one another if we consciously acknowledged that each of us is B'Tzelem Elohim, a reflection of the image of God.

My friend Susan practices what Judaism calls *Gemilut Hasidim*, acts of loving kindness. The rabbis considered

God to be the Originator of acts of loving kindness, the most notable of which are acts for which there is no hope of being rewarded, such as burying the dead. Simply put, it is goodness done for goodness' sake.

In her continuing efforts to pay attention to the "little" things in life, Susan has caused me to realize something important. It is not the devil that resides in the details, but God's Divine presence. For it is in the smallest acts of kindness that we can find some of the grandest aspects of humanity. How much kinder a place the world would be if we could slow down just a little bit to appreciate this bit of wisdom.

Gratitude: A Pathway to Happiness

It is early in the morning, traffic is terrible, and I am racing across town to make it to my 7:30 yoga class on time. As I run panting into the room, I smile at the irony of entering a space where mindfulness of breath is at the heart of the practice. I sit on my mat, close my eyes and chant the OM with the others in my class. My breathing becomes noticeably slower although my mind is still bouncing around, wondering if I locked my car and turned off my cell phone.

My teacher reads a poem by Robert Louis Stevenson and asks us to dedicate our yoga practice today to something that is important to us. I drink in a long breath, feeling the air circulate up through my nose, spreading deep into my lungs. I release a long, slow exhale, aware that less than a year ago I was unable to do this. The sinus surgery I had dreaded made it possible for me to now breathe fully. The word GRATITUDE enters my mind.

Gratitude is appreciation for what we have that is good in our lives. From the moment we wake up in the morning, we have things to be grateful for. A good night's rest in a warm bed, waking up in a safe place, a job to go to or a family to feed. Simple things that we often overlook and take for granted.

In Hebrew, the word for gratitude is *hakarat ha tov*, which means 'recognition of the good,' especially of the good things that others have done for us. Hakarat ha tov is meant to make us feel good about ourselves. It requires us to stop, look around and remember the times in our life when others were there for us because they cared about or appreciated us. When we recognize that a busy friend set aside time to help us or that a supervisor has promoted us because she values our work, we feel worthy, valued and loved. When we cultivate gratitude, we move closer to becoming a happier person.

I love the word gratitude because it contains another word within it (although slightly misspelled) which is at the heart of gratitude itself: Attitude. So much of whether we feel grateful for things lies in our attitude about life. Everyone experiences difficult times: poor health, financial problems or family strife can make it very hard to feel upbeat and grateful. While we can't always choose what happens to us, we can choose how we feel about it and how we respond. As my father says: "When things are tough, you can have a good attitude or a bad one for the same nickel."

Gratitude requires us to make the choice to be conscious of what we have, rather than what we lack. It asks us to see the glass as half full rather than half empty. One way to develop gratitude is to take time each day to acknowledge what we have that is good in our life at that very moment. Then, and this is the hard part, to say it aloud—to ourselves and to others to whom we are grateful. It may be as simple as acknowledging that we have just read a good book or thanking a teacher for a wonderful class or telling a friend how happy we are to have lunch with her. It is this conscious and articulated awareness of what we have that can bring us joy for the daily blessings in our lives.

The Jewish tradition tells us that we should say 100 blessings every day. Some are traditional blessings that we say upon waking, eating and praying. Others are spontaneous and require us to stay open to the good around us that deserves our praise. Articulating what we are grateful for is a *mitzvah* because it is tantamount to saying a blessing.

My teacher ends class with the chanting of the OM and I sit, head bowed, grateful that I chose to start my day with yoga. As I roll up my mat and head back to the car, the words of the poem she read to us come back to me.

"The best things are nearest you: breath in your nostrils, light in your eyes, flowers at your feet, duties at your hand and the path of God just before you."

Five blessings right there. I feel happier already!

To Err Is to Be Human; to Forgive, Nearly Impossible

On a chilly day in February several years ago, I drove my mother to the hospital to visit her only sister, Emily. My mother was, as always, anxious about seeing her. Not just because of her condition, which was bordering on terminal, but because of their relationship, defined by years of unspoken hurt and unfinished conversations.

We both fidgeted in the elevator as we approached the room to say what we anticipated were our final goodbyes. No matter how hard you try, there is no way to prepare for a moment like this. You can intellectually comfort yourself with thoughts like "She's so sick, it's for the best," or "She's lived a good life and now it's her time." But as we entered the room I was struck by the realization that the cadaverous shell of a woman lying in bed, the same woman who had caused my mother so much pain in her youth, might never be able to speak again. And there was still so much left to say.

Her daughter greeted us at the door.

"She's been calling for you for days," she said softly, looking at my mother.

My mother's discomfort permeated the room. Unclear how to act and unsure of what to say, she tried at first to be upbeat and optimistic, brightly suggesting that perhaps more time and a new medication might make a difference. But her sister's unfocused gaze and low, continuous moans punctuated each word and soon my mother stopped talking.

Something inside me knew that Emily recognized that Mom had come, so I bent over my mother, who stood frozen by her side, and whispered into her ear.

"Hold her hand, Mom, and stroke it so she knows that you're here. Tell her you love her; just tell her that it's okay."

Which is exactly what Mom did. And when she began touching Emily's forehead with her own tired hand, Emily looked up and SAW. She SAW and she KNEW, as clearly as I knew, that it was my mother, her sister. A smile spread slowly across Emily's face and for a few moments, her weary eyes were young again.

My mother kept repeating softly, "I love you Emily. I really love you." And Emily, who had been unable to talk for days, uttered the words which have helped to heal my mother's pain and teach her how to forgive: "I love you too, Elise. I have always loved you."

Granting forgiveness to those who have hurt us is one of the most difficult things to do: it doesn't come easily or naturally for most of us. The emotional, psychological and spiritual strength that it takes to forgive someone who owes us love and affection but instead hurts, abandons or betrays us challenges even the most "forgiving" of people.

Because when we are wronged, the natural tendency is to withdraw, become hostile or vindictive, all of which lead to increased strain in the very relationship we need to work on.

There is profound wisdom in the Jewish tradition about the human capacity to forgive. We are taught that we can't seek forgiveness from anyone other than the person we have hurt. For that, not even God can forgive us. Instead, we must ask forgiveness directly from the offended person and, if after three attempts we are still not forgiven, our obligation is satisfied.

When we are wronged, the Torah counsels us not to take vengeance or to bear a grudge. (Leviticus 19:18) We are inspired by our Talmudic sages who taught that when we forgive the sins of others, we will likewise be forgiven for our own sins. (Megillah 28a)

There is a lovely prayer called the Bedtime *Shema*, which is traditionally recited before retiring each evening. In it, we explicitly forgive anyone who has angered, antagonized or hurt us that day by speech, deed or thought— regardless of whether it was accidental and careless or willful and purposeful. Each night we are reminded that to be human is to err, but to forgive brings us closer to the Divine.

I think of the years of hurt that my mother endured and of how she longed for her sister to acknowledge and apologize for the wrongs she had done, or at least to talk about them. She will never have that conversation now, but what she does have is almost as good. She was able to put her own anger aside long enough to have a final, connecting moment where the bond of two sisters prevailed. And in doing so, she found a path to forgiveness and a way to remember her sister with love.

Spiritual Nourishment for Our Families

What Should We Name Our Baby?

I never realized I wanted a Hebrew name until I lived in Israel during my junior year of college. The first day of class, my teacher asked us our names. As student after student answered, I began to feel somewhat confused. Why did all these American college kids have romantic biblical names like Miriam, Aaron and Tamar when I only had plain, old-fashioned Amy?

I knew my name had meaning, especially to my mother who named me Beth Amy after her two favorite characters in *Little Women*. But in that classroom of beautiful Hebrew names, I was an anomaly. I turned to my friend Lisa and asked her how she came to be called Rivka.

"My English name is Lisa Anne, but my parents named me Rivka Leah in Hebrew to honor both of my grandmothers."

I was sweating by the time it was my turn. I thought of making up a name but blurted out the truth instead.

"I don't have a Hebrew name," I practically whimpered.

"Let's give you one, then," she responded with a smile.

The power of naming dates back to Biblical times when we learn that Adam's first independent act was to name the animals. In the Book of Genesis, when a person's name is changed it signifies spiritual development and enlightenment—such as when Abram and Sarai are renamed Abraham and Sarah after they accept God's covenant and when Jacob is renamed Israel after he struggles with an angel and receives his blessing.

Naming our children is the very first thing we do to give them an identity. In the Jewish tradition, a boy customarily receives his Hebrew name on the eighth day after his birth at the ceremony of the circumcision or *Brit Milah*. A girl is often named in synagogue on a day when the Torah is read in a celebration called the *Bat Simcha*.

In our family, we created a special baby naming ceremony in our home for each child, to which we invited family and friends. With our children wrapped in the *tallit* that we used for the canopy of our wedding *huppah*, we shared the reasons why we chose the names we did and blessed our children by planting trees in their honor. Over the years, we have watched those trees grow and flourish and are reminded with each passing season of our commitment to create a Jewish home and life.

While there are no laws on Jewish baby naming, there is an abundance of customs, folklore and superstitions. I found this out when we talked about naming my son after his Grandma Edna, who was alive at the time. When I told her my idea, she blanched, shook her head and made a clucking sound with her tongue. I didn't know that among Ashkenazic Jews, it is forbidden to

31

name a child after a living relative because of the super-stition that a name carries special powers. If you name a child after a living relative, it is feared that he or she will die sooner or that you will bring bad luck to your child.

Sephardic Jews have a contrary belief, however, and often name a baby after a living relative explicitly to honor them. Since my mother is Sephardic and I felt comfortable following both traditions, we chose a Solo-monic-like solution and named my son after my deceased grandfather and my mother, who proudly held him at the ceremony.

Hebrew names are most often used in a religious context and for Jewish life cycle events. When we read from the Torah, sign a marriage contract, pray for the speedy recovery of someone and recite the Mourner's Kaddish, we use Hebrew names. And, as I learned on my first day in class at Hebrew University, when we study with other Jews we use one as well.

There are many wonderful names to choose from, including over 2,000 found in the Bible. Or you may want to consult from one of the many contemporary books on the subject. A good place to start is with "The New Jewish Baby Book: Names, Ceremonies, Customs—A Guide for Today's Families" by Anita Diamant or "The Complete Book of Hebrew Baby Names" by Smadar Shir Sidi.

My teacher asked me my English name and her eyes lit up when I told her.

"How lovely!" she responded. "We can use that for your Hebrew name as well."

Today I am proud to call myself Bat Ami (from Beth Amy) which means Daughter of My People. It is a name that inspires me to stay connected to the Jewish community and reminds me of my unique relationship with God.

And You Shall Teach Your Children

Years ago, when my husband and I began searching for a house for our growing family, we didn't really care about the height of the ceilings or the size of the master bath. Our top priority was finding a home in a safe neighborhood with good schools nearby. Just when we thought we couldn't look at one more "darling kitchen-in-need-of-repair," we found it. Nestled in a cul-de-sac within walking distance from an elementary school, I knew it would be a wonderful place to raise our family.

I marvel at how important safety has become to me now that I am a parent. As cavalier as I was in my hitch-hiking college days, I now am a full-fledged member of the Society of the Permanently Vigilant. From the search for lead-free, non-flammable toys that filled our play room to the caution we took in choosing movies and computer games, our every thought has been to keep our children safe. But how can we keep them safe when we don't even know what or whom they invite into their rooms from the world of cyberspace? And how do we avoid overprotecting our children and burdening them with our fears so that we don't stunt their curiosity and inhibit their growth, self-sufficiency and independence?

I ask serious and complex questions for which there are no simple or guaranteed answers. But for as long as there have been children, there have been parents who worry about them. And Jewish tradition has one of the most practical and common sense responses to these concerns that I have yet to find. For at the heart of all Jewish parenting is the commandment to "Teach your children" and an obligation to be a moral role model and guide.

In Hebrew the home is called *Mikdash Ma'at*, or little sanctuary, and is considered a sacred place; one where love, learning and the transmission of values takes place. Ideally, it is where a child develops a sense of identity, self-worth and a feeling of belonging to something greater than just him or her self. As parents, it is up to us to decide which tools to use to enrich our families and bring joy, meaning, knowledge and values into our home and families. As Jews, we are blessed with a treasure chest of traditions, holidays and rituals from which to choose to help us in this formidable task.

The Hebrew word for parents, *horeem*, comes from the word "teacher." We are designated as the teachers of tradition, responsible for connecting our children to their faith while permitting them to question and challenge what they do not understand. If we are not capable or do not know how to teach them ourselves, we can turn to family members, friends, teachers and rabbis for help.

The Talmud tells us that we are required to teach our children Torah so that they can choose well and live moral and spiritually meaningful lives. We must teach them a vocation so that they can become financially independent. We must help them choose a suitable life partner so that they can live emotionally fulfilling lives. And we must instruct them to swim, so that they will feel secure in their physical surroundings.

There is a concept in Judaism called *tzar gidul banim* (literally, the *tzures,* or sorrow, of growing children) which is axiomatic of the parent-child relationship. Simply put, tzar gidul banim recognizes that all parents suffer some amount of anxiety, unhappiness, tension, and worry while raising their children. What Jewish parenting wisdom tells us is that if we do our job and teach our children well, and if we let them exercise their free will (within reason), they will ultimately learn to choose right from wrong. This insight recognizes that children often learn to make better choices as a result of having made poorer ones.

Even if we do our job as parent-teachers, there is something more we must have as parents. My mother calls its *mazel,* and several parenting books I've read say it's patience, tough-love or both. But I would call it faith—in ourselves, our children and God—that even when our best efforts do not immediately produce the results we hope for, our children will learn to work things out for themselves over time.

Showing Our Children How to Give from the Heart

As a child, I hated having my birthday fall in the middle of December because it meant that no matter when Chanukah began, my birthday gifts were somehow expected to count for Chanukah too. It just didn't seem fair that I had to give up some of my gifts because of a glitch in the calendar.

I never told anyone about my frustration though, except perhaps a therapist or two along the way. But recently I heard a story from my friend Rachel about her daughter, Hannah, who also shares the December birthday dilemma, which gave me a new insight about birthday gifts and giving.

After Hannah's third birthday party, Rachel surveyed the room and realized that among the decorations and left-over cake were enough presents to fill a small toy store. And it bothered her that her own child should have so much when there were so many others who have so little. So she came up with a plan that was both ingenious and Jewish-minded to the core.

She told Hannah about all of the children who lived in Tucson who didn't have any toys for their birthdays or

Chanukah and asked her what she thought they could do to help. With some "gentle parental maneuvering," it didn't take long for Hannah to suggest that she give up a present from the pile on the floor. Hannah chose a Care Bear and then, after a few moments, picked out a talking doll and a child's tea set and together, mother and daughter re-wrapped the gifts.

A few days later, Rachel drove Hannah to Jewish Family and Children's Service with the presents. When Rachel arrived, she asked a staff person if she would tell Hannah about the families who needed the presents and how much it would mean to the children who received them. A few weeks later when Rachel drove past the JFCS building, Hannah looked up in recognition and asked her mom, "Do you think the kids are playing with my Care Bear right now?" Rachel nodded and smiled. It was one of those rare and precious moments when being the parent of a toddler seems like the easiest thing in the world.

Tzedakah, the Jewish responsibility to give to others in need, is often described as charity. But the word itself comes from the Hebrew word *Tzedek*, or justice, and is based on the Biblical commandment: "If there is a needy person among you…you shall not harden your heart or close your hand against him." (Deut. 15:7) Giving to others is not optional: It is one way Jews are mandated to pursue justice in the world.

The Jewish obligation to give applies to all of us, regardless of our social or financial status. The Rabbis were clear that even a person in need should find a way to give to others when they taught: "Even a poor man who himself survives on charity should give charity." (Babylonian Talmud, *Gittin* 7B)

Rachel's family began to put money in a Tzedakah box every Friday night before Shabbat and Hannah knew that the box was for the people who didn't have toys or food or a place to live. When Hannah was five, she saw pictures of the victims of Hurricane Katrina on television and came running into the kitchen to find Rachel. "Mommy," she asked in a worried voice, "don't we need to give our money to the children in the hurricane?" Rachel emptied out the Tzedakah box and took Hannah to the Jewish Federation with over 80 dollars in change.

It is difficult, almost impossible, to convey to our children how horrible it is for others who live in poverty, and don't have families, friends or resources to turn to for help. Not only is the concept foreign to their lives, but it runs counter to contemporary expectations in today's youth culture of buying more, owning more and having more. Yet we can start at an early age, as Rachel did with Hannah, by modeling our values and teaching our children the responsibility we have as Jews to care for those in need. And in doing so, we will empower our children with the awareness that they too can do something, at every age and stage of life, to make the world a better place.

Finding New Ways to Honor Our Parents

My Dad has always been a larger-than-life type of guy. For most of my childhood, he was the dominant force in our family, even though Mom often manipulated the outcome from behind the curtains like the Wizard of Oz. When a tired and grumpy Dad came home from work, my brother and I knew better than to disturb him until dinner. We would tip-toe past the den, where Dad had retreated in solitude to open the mail or take a power nap in his leather recliner, the newspaper tented over his face.

Dad would come to the dinner table and sit in "his" chair—a place that none of us dreamed of sitting in—and talk about his day. Between mouthfuls of chicken and corn, I learned about grown-up things like office equipment, stocks and bonds and the stresses of working in a family business. Without a doubt, dinner was my favorite time of day.

I didn't know then that not sitting in my father's chair was particularly Jewish, but I have since learned that refraining from sitting in a parent's place is one of the ways we traditionally honor our parents. The two texts in the Torah that tell us what obligations are expected of children are: The Fifth Commandment (Exodus 20:12) to "*honor* your father and mother" and Leviticus 19:3, to "*revere* your mother and father." Honor and reverence are two concepts of duty, requiring different sensitivities and commitments on our part as children.

To honor is deemed a positive *mitzvah* requiring us to provide food, clothing, shelter and for the physical needs of a parent in much the same way they provided for us when we were young. To revere is viewed as a negative commandment, requiring us to refrain from doing certain things, like sitting in our parent's chair or contradicting or humiliating them in public. (Teenagers take note!) These obligations extend to all children, whether biological, adopted or step, but there are certain exceptions to the rule. If a parent requires a child to violate a commandment, forbids a child to go to Israel, forces a marriage partner, causes strife between a child and his or her spouse or is evil, wicked or abusive, then that child is released from the commandment to honor and revere the offending parent.

It is fascinating to me that nowhere in the Torah are we required to *love* our parents, only to honor and revere them. Why not command love for our parents when we are commanded to love others like our neighbors and strangers? One interpretation is that it isn't necessary to state that we should love our parents because it is such an obvious, primary and natural response. Another interpretation, which shows remarkable insight and wisdom on the part of our sages, suggests that for some people, loving our parents may be an impossible request. The obligations of the Torah are designed for us to be able to fulfill. Commanding us to love our parents is something we may not be able to do because it is based on how we feel. Honoring our parents is possible, however, regardless of how we feel, because it is based on our actions, not our feelings.

I would like to offer an additional way to honor our parents, one that requires nothing but our time, interest and willingness to listen. For many of us who are still lucky enough to have living parents, there is no better time than the present to ask them about their lives and their stories. When we ask our parents to share their stories, we do much to honor them. Expressing who they are and what they value most not only helps them make sense of their lives but proves that they mattered and that their lives have lasting meaning.

Listening to our parents' stories gives us an opportunity to slow ourselves down and create sacred time to honor them by showing them that we care. It may be difficult or awkward at first but you can start with some general questions that will open the door to deeper conversation. Questions like: What have been the most important things in your life? What values have affected your decisions? What people influenced you the most? What regrets do you have? What are your hopes for your children and grandchildren?

In our fast-paced, future-oriented society, where things become obsolete before we have even taken them out of the box, the world needs the wisdom of our parents, whose love, values and stories can inspire us to live more meaningful lives as we face an uncertain future.

Five Gold Bangles and
a World of Difference

The morning of my wedding day, my mother called me into her bedroom. "Come sit with me," she said quietly, patting the spot next to her on the bed.

I sat down beside her, the softness of the mattress causing our shoulders to touch.

She turned her face toward mine, looking happier than I had seen her look in years. I attributed it to the fact that her almost-thirty-year-old daughter was finally getting married. Smiling, she handed me a box.

"Open it," she urged.

Inside the box were five beautiful, gold-filigree bangle bracelets of different patterns. The gold was unlike any I had ever seen and the bracelets warmed as I held them in my hands. They were not new, their shapes having been altered from perfect circles to imperfect ones by the wrists they had adorned.

I turned them over in my hands and, one by one, slid them on my right arm. They were truly lovely.

"Oh, Mom, I love them! Where did you get them?"

She answered by telling me a story about my great-grandmother, Jamilla Danino, who, at the age of 12, married a man more than three times her age to become his second wife. Born in 1882 to a poor family in Alexandria, Egypt, she had no choice but to respect the arrangement her parents had made. One afternoon he arrived with gifts, and a week later she left on a ship with her new husband for Haifa, never to see her parents again. The bracelets on my arm were the same ones that Jamilla had received from her husband as an engagement gift.

Living in the 21st century it is hard to fathom an arrangement like the one Jamilla's parents made for her. I barely get to meet the boys my daughter, Lauren, dates, let alone have the deciding vote as to whom. And I quiver at the idea that I might never see Lauren again or be able to cuddle my grandchildren on my lap.

Yet as recently as the early 1900s, my great-grandmother was forced to live side by side with the other woman who shared her husband's bed but could not give him a child. For Sephardic Jews who lived in communities influenced by Islam, like Egypt, Yemen, Morocco and Turkey, a polygamous marriage like Jamilla's was an accepted practice.

The Bible is filled with stories of unhappiness and the problems that exist in a polygamous marriage: Sarah was derided by Hagar because she couldn't have a child, Leah was jealous of Rachel because Jacob loved her more, and Solomon's many wives brought idolatry into the land of Israel. Jamilla suffered a similar fate when, at the tender age of 13, she gave birth to a son, Albert. She was scorned by the first wife and suffered terribly at her hands. What saved Jamilla during those difficult years was her wit, wisdom and undying love for her son, my grandfather.

The laws on polygamy, which often created hardship and injustice for women throughout Jewish history, have thankfully changed. In Eastern Europe, Rabbi Gershom decreed a ban on polygamy in the 10th century but Sephardic Jews did not accept it. When Israel was created in 1948, in order to accommodate its Sephardic immigrants, the government honored existing polygamous marriages but forbad future ones. Today, the ban on polygamy is universally accepted in the Jewish world.

I treasure wearing my gold bracelets for many reasons. They help me remember my great-grandmother, a woman whose courage, strength and devotion carried her through a lifetime of struggle. They remind me of my mother, who wore them as a young girl when she was raised by Jamilla as a result of her own parents' untimely deaths. And they give me a sense of optimism about our future as Jews. For it is through the wisdom of the Jewish tradition and its ability to change laws that are patently unfair or result in hardship and injustice, that our greatest hope for the future lies.

Everyone Has a Story to Tell

L ast year my mother turned 80, and we celebrated with a family trip to Montana. The gift she cherished most was not the picture frame we had engraved or even the matching bracelets I made for all the women in the family. It was simply being surrounded by her family, laughing, toasting and sharing memories and stories together.

But afterward, a sort of gloominess set in as Mom experienced a letdown after her Big Event. It was evident in our daily phone conversations as she recited a litany of new complaints: Her book group was boring, all of her friends were sick or moving to Florida, her doctor never called her back.

"You need something to do, Mom, something to focus on to keep you excited about life," I told her with the certainty of a psychiatrist. "There's still a lot out there for you. Why don't you take a class, start painting again or write about your life?"

Mom responded to the last idea like a flower in need of water. Since I live more than 2,000 miles away, I gave her a "crash phone course" on how to use Google to research where she might find a writing class. She called a friend and they began to plan it together. The friend, she confided to me, didn't even *like* Florida and was staying put for the winter. Within a few days, they had both enrolled in "Writing Your Memoirs" and what transpired over the next 10 weeks is a story in itself.

The first week she called me daily—not with complaints but with questions about how to use "this darn machine" to make it do what she wanted. When my long distance computer tutoring didn't do the trick, I told her to go to her local library where they have tutoring for free.

My mother is not a technically gifted person, but what she lacks in mechanical skills she more than makes up in willful determination. At the library she met a retired woman who volunteered to come to her house to help her. What started out as a lesson in Microsoft Word blossomed into a lovely friendship as my mother and her new friend began to share their lives over Diet Coke and the keyboard.

As the semester unfolded, I heard a renewed energy in Mom's voice. She would call and tell me about the dream she had of a childhood friend or a memory about her father walking through the apartment where they lived when she was 2 years old. Because my mother lost both of her parents just before her third birthday, the stories she has been told about them were crucial to her sense of being. In her darkest moments, it was stories about her family that kept the pieces of her life together. Writing about them now did much to bring renewed meaning to her days and a sense of peace to her life.

Without our stories we are drifters: they act as anchors in the turbulent waters of our lives. But stories, like water, are fluid. Each time one is repeated, something is changed. A small detail is added, a few words are left out, a name once lost is remembered. What matters most is not that the facts are true but that the deeper truths within the stories are revealed.

My mother sent me a folder with the work she submitted for her final class. She wrote in the voice of Jamilla, the grandmother who raised her after both of her parents died. As I read them with a lump in my throat that refused to recede, I found these truths: That no matter how lost or lonely we may be, when we feel loved and connected to family, we can survive the worst of times. And it is through the discovery and sharing of our stories with others—be they our children, grandchildren, or friends—that we can appreciate the meaning of our life and let our life have continued meaning.

Embracing Change: Welcome Transformations in My Family and Faith

I sit at my computer with a coffee mug and my cell phone on silent for a while. Generally, I don't move from my seat until my first draft is completed but today I keep getting up—to water the plants, fix a snack, check the mail. I have the writing jitters, which surprises me as I thought I had become immune to feeling vulnerable when I share my life with my readers. This story is different however, and I wonder about how to write it and even whether I should write it at all.

Because with these words I am officially coming out of the closet; not as a lesbian myself, but as the mother of a gay son. It's taken me a while to "out" myself, primarily out of respect for my son's privacy and the fact that it should be him, and not me, who decides if, when and to whom to disclose his sexual orientation. But he has been gracious and bold enough to give me permission to write this story, in the hopes that what I write may open the hearts and minds of others.

Joshua came out to his dad and me the night before he left for college. We were not surprised; in fact, we were deeply grateful and relieved. Grateful that he trusted us enough to tell us, and relieved because we suspected he was gay for many years and it was wonderful not have to dance around the topic any more. For me this meant I could stop leaving magazines lying open to stories about gay marriage or the threat of HIV. For Joshua, it meant that he could begin to live his life out in the open, regardless of whether he was at home or at school.

"Out of the closet and into the street!" was one of the first rallying cries of the gay civil rights movement. Yet being openly gay requires giving up something we all value: our privacy. It means that your sexuality is a topic that others can, and most likely will, discuss—and often in unkind ways. Even if this openness has helped our society become more aware that many of the people we know and care about are gay, there is an undeniable social stigma for those who admit to being part of the LGBT (lesbian/gay/bisexual/transgender) community.

I grew up in a home where homosexuality was never discussed until I brought my best friend, Rick, home from college over winter break and learned the ugly meaning of the Yiddish word "fagelah." My parents and I parted ways, with me fuming at what I saw as their ignorance and prejudice and them worrying that they had sent me to a college far too liberal for my own good. I was convinced that my father was homophobic and I was probably right, given the period in which he grew up and the prevailing attitudes of his time. And while he claimed to have several "fagelah friends" who were in the theatre when he was in college, I sensed his deep discomfort whenever he talked about them.

After Joshua came out, we asked him how he felt about us telling others that he was gay. He said it was fine with him, but then hesitated and said: "But I don't want you to tell Grandpa, because I'm afraid it will change the way he feels about me."

I nodded with a lump in my throat thinking, "Some things don't have to be said to be understood."

Time passed and I could tell my parents suspected Joshua was gay. A year or so later I asked Joshua if he still felt the same about me not telling his grandfather. I knew that my father adored him, that he admired his intellect, curiosity and unique spirit. And Joshua must have known that too because he told me it was okay to tell him. And I did.

I began the conversation somewhat defensively, expecting to find the old dad of my college years responding to what I had to say. But when I told him that Joshua was gay, he responded simply and without hesitation.

"I love my grandson and as far as I'm concerned, his sexuality is a non-issue."

And that was the end of the conversation. Thirty-five years and a grandson later, my father opened his mind and heart to loving someone so completely that he was able to set aside his previous feelings in order to stay close to Joshua. I sat still, moved beyond words, to be a witness to this transformation. Anything that I might have harbored against my dad, the pain and injustices of my own youth, was forgiven in an instant of his unconditional love.

But it is not only my own father who has changed. Thankfully, I can now look at the Jewish tradition and say that it, too, has evolved over time to acknowledge the reality of homosexuality as a way of life and part of the human condition.

Judaism's traditional position on homosexuality is based on two verses in the Torah that condemn the male homosexual act as an "abomination," or *toevah* in Hebrew. (Leviticus 18:22 and 20:13) While the Torah does not prohibit lesbian sex, later rabbinic commentators have condemned it as "indecent" and "immodest" behavior. It is important to note that nowhere in Jewish sources is the person who is a homosexual condemned, only the homosexual act itself. While this may not be a great comfort to a gay man who wants sexual intimacy with another man, liberal Jews have fully embraced gays and lesbians as congregants and leaders.

Jewish law or *Halacha* is the path that we are expected to follow in order to be closer to God and one another. Its foundation lies in the wisdom, laws and admonitions of the Torah, which are more fully interpreted by the Talmud and other rabbinic sources. But the laws of the Torah are meant for us to live by, not to die for or be unable to fulfill as a result of being human.

Some think that Orthodox Jewish law does not or cannot change. This is not the case, however, as anyone familiar with Jewish history or Talmud will affirm.

When social, economic and political conditions shift, when scientific realities are uncovered, Jewish law has been "re-applied" to ensure the proper commitment to the Torah's original purposes. Legal rulings concerning marriage, divorce, slavery, inheritance, mourning rituals and relations with non-Jews have all changed over time. It is Judaism's ongoing commitment to both tradition and change that have kept it alive, meaningful and relevant over the past two thousand years. And while this commitment may vary in degree among the different streams of Judaism, it is present in all of them.

For many years, the Reform, Reconstructionist and Renewal movements have recognized homosexual relationships and have permitted their rabbis to officiate at same-sex commitment/marriage ceremonies. In addition, they have admitted openly homosexual candidates into their rabbinical and cantorial schools, ordaining gay and lesbian clergy throughout the country.

On December 6, 2006, after years of debate, the Conservative movement voted to permit the ordination of openly gay and lesbian rabbinical students and permit same-sex unions. The decision was based on the Jewish commitment to pluralism, which recognizes that there is more than one way of authentically following our tradition and still be considered a seriously engaged Jew. In a move exemplary of the Conservative movement's philosophy, it did not end the prior ban against gay unions, leaving individual rabbis and congregations to choose which ruling to follow.

I am the proud mother of a gay son and I am also a

proud Jew. Proud that my son is who he is and proud that my religious tradition has evolved in such a way to embrace every member of my family equally.

Ethical Wills: Ensuring
That Our Values Live On

I count myself among the most fortunate of "fifty-somethings," because both of my parents are still alive. Sometimes this weighs heavily on me, like when my mother leaves multiple messages on my answering machine because I haven't called her back—within the hour. Or when my father insists on driving me to the airport, even though his vision is so limited that I find myself praying silently most of the way. But I would take these "problems" any day of the week over the alternative, and relish hearing Dad answer the phone when I call, knowing that he will predictably hand it over to Mom to do the talking.

Recently I had one of the hardest conversations with my parents that any child could ever have. Despite my training as a lawyer and familiarity with estate planning, it quickly became clear to me that that no matter what age or stage of life you are in, talking to your parents about their wishes regarding death requires real emotional strength. Yet it is a conversation that is both important and necessary, because it gives parents an opportunity to express their desires and children a chance to question, understand and honor the values of their parents.

Jewish tradition teaches that it is a mitzvah "to carry out the directions of the deceased." This has been interpreted as creating a legal obligation when it comes to disposing of a parent's assets and possessions; similar to what would occur if the parent had written a Last Will and Testament. In addition, when a parent instructs a child on matters of his or her burial, these instructions are considered obligatory unless the request requires a child to violate Jewish law.

But there are certain directives which, while not legally mandated under Jewish law, are expected to be followed. For example, when a dying parent instructs a child not to cut off relations with other family members or tells him to avoid drinking excessively, Jewish law urges the child to honor his or her parent's wishes because they are intended to benefit the child. This is especially true when a parent's wishes are to ensure *shalom bayit*, or peace in the home.

When a parent provides moral guidance to a child, it is often with the hope that the values that the parent holds most dear will live on in their children and grandchildren. This idea, that values should be passed *L'Dor v Dor*, or from one generation to the next, has been formally recognized in Judaism through a lovely tradition called an "ethical will."

An ethical will is an informal, written document through which a parent bequests, not property or assets, but wisdom and values. It permits a parent to transmit an ethical legacy to his or her children through stories, examples and meaningful life lessons, in the hope that they will embrace those values in their own lives. It is meant to inspire, enlighten and encourage but never to punish, harass, blame or control a child "from the grave."

There are no formal requirements for writing an ethical will. You need only the desire to share what has been most important to you in your life, and some quiet time to record it. An ethical will can be written, typed, or, if a person is no longer able to write, recorded on a tape recorder. It can be written all at once or in segments, using life cycle events such as Bar Mitzvahs, graduations, weddings or the birth of a child as a time for reflection and composition. In some instances, it is appropriate to write a single ethical will for the entire family; in others, it may be wiser to write separate wills for each child. And, since an ethical will can be given to a child at any time during his or her life, a parent can decide when it will be most meaningful for the child to receive it.

An ethical will is a window to the soul; it provides a wonderful opportunity to share with our families the ideas, events, people and experiences that have shaped our lives and been important to us. It is a gift—both to ourselves and to our families—if we take the time to write one.

Learning through Living

Are You a Funnel or a Sponge?

When I first met my husband I thought he was very, very smart. I was worried that he would lose interest in me once he came to realize that I, on the other hand, had definite learning problems. I tried my best to hide this fact from him by quoting Op-Ed pieces from the New York Times and talking about complicated issues like global warming and world hunger. But it wasn't long before he found me out.

My intellectual undoing came in the form of simple, dead giveaways—like the fact that I can never find my location on a map even when it says in bold, red letters: "YOU ARE HERE." Or the tremendous problem I have trying to follow an instruction manual, which usually results in me returning the object, in multiple, broken parts, for store credit.

Notwithstanding my shortcomings, my husband married me anyway. As a result, he navigates most of our trips and never gives me a "do-it-yourself" gift. And I have come to appreciate and accept two basic premises about life: that intelligence and learning are in great measure a function of the way we process information and that everyone absorbs information differently.

I am not alone in this discovery. There are many who have elaborated upon the theory of "multiple intelligences," suggesting that there are a number of distinct forms of intelligence that each of us have to varying degrees. Howard Gardner, in his seminal book "Multiple Intelligences: The Theory in Practice" defines the seven types of intelligence as linguistic, musical, mathematical, spatial, body-kinesthetic, intrapersonal and interpersonal. And internationally acclaimed psychologist and author, Daniel Goleman, turned the concept of emotional intelligence into an accepted idea in American corporate and academic communities.

These theories imply that teaching and learning should focus on the particular intelligences each person has, rather than assume that everyone will learn in the same manner. For example, a person with strong spatial or musical intelligences should be encouraged to design buildings or compose music. In my case, I should never, ever be trusted as a wilderness guide or be given any serious responsibilities for home improvement. But if you want a story, I'm your gal!

What I find most astounding is that the idea of multiple intelligences dates back 2,000 years, to when the Talmudic rabbis developed their own, very cogent theory about how we absorb and process information. In *Ethics of the Fathers* (5:18) we are told: "There are four types of those that sit at the feet of the Sages: a sponge, a funnel, a strainer and a sieve. A sponge, which absorbs everything; a funnel, which lets in from one end and lets out from the other; a strainer, which lets the wine flow through and retains the sediment; and a sieve, which allows the flour dust to pass through and retains the fine flour."

There are various traditional interpretations of this passage, most of which relate to a person's ability to distinguish between truth and counterfeit, between what is meaningful and what is not. But given what we know about intelligence today, we can extend those interpretations a bit further to help us become better Jewish educators with more gratified Jewish students.

Looking at the four types of students, we can see that each person has a unique character that will influence learning. A sponge absorbs everything and will most likely be a quick learner. For this student, we may need to provide continual inspiration and challenges to keep him stimulated. The funnel may not retain information as well and may need more experiential, hands-on learning rather than traditional textbook teaching to integrate the material. The strainer lets certain material go, keeping only the larger, more salient facts at hand. He or she may be the global thinker, one who enjoys studying the macro-issues and defining concepts. Finally, the sieve absorbs, synthesizes and refines the material, depicting the finest of details and nuances. This student may benefit from opportunities to refine his ideas through the art of debate, writing and text analysis. From the standpoint of providing quality Jewish education today, we can profit from acknowledging that students enter the classroom with different learning strengths, weaknesses and tendencies. Let us stop and be thankful for these differences and hope that all teachers, from preschool to adult education, learn to appreciate and work with them. Because only then will we be able to meet the greatest challenge of Jewish education—to inspire, enable and empower students to integrate Jewish learning into their hearts and lives.

I Was Cursed to Be a Teacher

I am not a superstitious person but believe me when I tell you I was cursed at the age of 10. Sitting at my small wooden desk in Mrs. Kennedy's fourth grade class, I had just finished showing Jessica Butler how to do long addition and was tidying up my papers before going out to recess. A dark shadow spread over my desk and I looked up into the chins, yes chins, of my teacher. I couldn't help but notice the wiry, black hair which seemed so out of place on a chin. Embarrassed, I looked down into her sturdy, sensible shoes. Was I in trouble for helping Jessica? Did she think I cheated on our spelling test?

"Amy, I've been watching you all year long," she began, "and I'm sure that you should become a teacher, just like me. You're a natural for it," she concluded, patting my head with her chalky fingertips.

I wasn't sure at the time if this was a compliment or an insult, seeing as in addition to the chins and the shoes, Mrs. Kennedy had big, drapery-like arms that swayed when she wrote on the blackboard.

That curse haunted me all through college and law school. Every time I turned around, someone asked me to teach. The local synagogue wanted me to teach Hebrew school. My kids' teachers wanted me to do the Jewish holidays. And then, one day, I got a phone call from the owner of a real estate school who wanted me to teach contract law to real estate agents. It sounded like fun and a good way to build my law practice, so I said yes.

I entered the classroom a bit nervous, more about the possibility that a stray chin hair might pop out than the likelihood that I wouldn't keep the agents engaged for the next three hours. It didn't take more than a few months however, to realize that Mrs. Kennedy was right. I absolutely loved being a teacher.

Several years into teaching, I had an epiphany while lecturing about the intricacies of contract default provisions and boiler plate clauses. How would it be to teach something I really, truly *cared* about? What would it be like to talk about matters of substance and really explore them with my students? The idea pulled at me and wouldn't let go.

Three years and a major illness later, I enrolled in a Master's degree program in Jewish studies, a decision that has changed my adult life more than any other choice I have made.

Over the past decade, I have had the privilege and the pleasure of teaching children, college students and adults about subjects and issues that truly matter to me as a Jewish woman, mother, wife, daughter, professional and community member. From Jewish ethics, spirituality and law to Jewish rituals, holidays and life-cycle events, there is nothing I teach that doesn't speak to me directly and personally. Each time I prepare for a class, whether it is a course on Jewish literature or one about the Jewish views on organ donation, I am energized and inspired by the Jewish texts that inform me as a teacher and guide me as an adult.

The one thing that Mrs. Kennedy never told me is how important my students would become to me—that they would not only become my friends but my teachers as well. A class doesn't go by that I don't learn something new from my students. I am inspired by the different ways they think, question, analyze and respond to the material I present. I am challenged by their critiques and questions and motivated by their interests and concerns. Simply put, my students have done more collectively to expand my set of assumptions and world views than any one teacher I have ever had.

My appreciation for my students is not unique. In fact, it is very Jewish. More than two thousand years ago, the sages recognized the significance of the role that a student plays in the life of his or her teacher when they said: "Much wisdom I learned from my teachers, more from my colleagues, but from my pupils, most of all."

I was cursed at the age of 10 to be a teacher—but in that role, I am truly blessed.

Discovering a "JEM"
in an Arizona Cave

I was ecstatic when our dear friends Barry and Bonnie called to tell us they were coming for a visit. Like most people, my husband and I rarely make time to do the wonderful "touristy" things in Tucson that others travel thousands of miles to see. So I immediately rushed to the phone to reserve a spot for the four of us for a tour at the world-renown caves located in southern Arizona.

It was a glorious day, and as we waited on the patio for the tour group to gather, our guide asked each of us where we were from.

"I live in San Diego now but I grew up in Oak Park, Michigan," Barry answered with a smile.

"Isn't that the place they call Jewtown? You know, the place where all the Jews live?" our guide asked.

I stood frozen in my disbelief, but without missing a beat, Barry answered him with the kind of clarity and calmness usually found in an operating room.

"I'm one of 'those Jews' and I am offended by your comment."

Our guide was truly bewildered. "But why?" he asked in earnest. "I had lots of Jewish friends when I lived in

68

Detroit and when we would drive past Oak Park, they told me that's what it's called."

"Well they were very wrong to say that," Barry answered, and we walked toward the tram that would take us to the cave.

Despite this unsettling beginning, the caves were magnificent and the tour guide did a good job describing the wonders within. At the end of the tour, Barry went to find the guide and thank him for the time he spent with us. I'll admit it; the word *mentsch* did cross my mind.

Like children on the playground, we huddled around Barry to find out what had happened.

"What did he say, what did he say?" we all wanted to know.

"He really felt badly about what he said, and had no idea that it was offensive. And he thanked me for telling him," Barry concluded as we entered the gift shop.

We saw amazing natural beauty that day; rooms with icicle-like stalactites 20 feet long and sheets of translucent rock formations that looked like giant shields. But the one JEM I didn't expect that afternoon was the one Barry helped me discover.

A JEM is a term I use to describe a "Jewish Educational Moment." Like an epiphany, a JEM is a novel insight or awareness that emerges from everyday living. It most often appears when you are confronted with a dilemma or issue and have absolutely no idea how to react, but suddenly, someone says or does something that gives you more wisdom than you would get from an hour of therapy.

Barry did not know it but he taught all of us many things that day. He taught our guide that using references like "Jewtown" is *de facto* offensive; it is a racial insult regardless of whether it is spoken by a Jew or a non-Jew. He taught me how effective it is to respond calmly when you are the subject of a racial slur. The simple but incontrovertible statement: "I am one of those Jews, and I am offended by that" will forever be etched in my mind as a mantra to use when I find myself in a similar situation.

And he showed all of us how important it is to be a mentsch. That once we make it clear that words like "Jewtown," "Indian-giver," and "fag" are inappropriate and hurtful, we can also be compassionate, forgiving and decent enough not to shame a person more than is necessary to make the point.

I also realized something very important: That as Jews, we must be careful not to make or use derogatory comments about ourselves, even in jest. Words like "Jewtown," when spoken by a Jew, legitimatize expressions that are disparaging and can encourage negative stereotyping, discrimination and hate.

I know our guide was upset about what he said and appreciated Barry for his candor and courtesy. The respect Barry gave him was also an indication of what it means to be a Jew. For in refraining from humiliating others and from not unfairly retaliating or bearing a grudge, we show the world a great deal about what is important to us as people and as Jews.

If Only I Could Stop the Clock Right Now

My daughter called from college the other day to share the happy news that she and her dance partner had won a Ballroom Dance competition. No one knew more than I how significant this was, coming from the same girl who had broken her back only three years before.

I hung up with a feeling of gratitude and drove to pick up the family pictures I had developed from my mother's 80th birthday celebration a few weeks before. I could hardly believe that the rosy-looking guy smiling back at me was my own father, the same man who spent most of last winter in the emergency room.

These events converge in my mind and make me understand more than ever the expression I heard when I was young: "If only I could stop the clock right now," my dad would muse, leaving the rest of the sentence unfinished.

But as Mark Twain wrote so eloquently, "Time and tide wait for no man," and no one can stop the forward motion of time and the events that will unfold. Yet the image of "stopping the clock" touches me because it invites me to appreciate just how lucky I am at this very moment in my life, while cautioning me to understand that invariably, things will change.

One of the most significant concepts in Judaism, which has preserved its unique way of life, is the idea of Jewish time; more specifically of time as presented in the Jewish calendar. The Jewish calendar is different from our secular calendar: it consists of 12 lunar months (except in a leap year when there are 13 months) or 354 days each year. Unlike the solar calendar, which is based on the 365 days it takes for the earth to fully circle the sun, the Jewish calendar is based on the 29 and one-half days it takes each month for the moon to circle the Earth.

As most Jews have come to realize, a lunar calendar poses certain challenges because holidays do not fall consistently on the same days each year. One year the first night of Hanukkah may be December 7th, and the next year it can fall on Christmas!

In order to prevent all of our holidays from running amuck so that we don't celebrate Passover in winter and Rosh Hashanah in the spring, we adjust the 11 day discrepancy between the solar and lunar calendars by adding a "leap month" seven times every 19 years. Talk about finding a creative solution to a difficult scientific problem—and this by the Talmudic sages over 2,000 years ago!

But Jewish time is more than what is contained in the calendar. It is unique in that it embraces the concept that time is both historical and cyclical; that time is spiritually grounded in the notion that we can see and feel God in both history and nature.

We are all familiar with historical time. It is the linear progression of time throughout our lives measured by clocks, calendars and anniversaries. We most often evaluate historical time in terms of progress; by the physical, intellectual, social and financial advances we make in our lives, by the growth of our children and by the developments in science, law and technology that change the way we live.

Cyclical time, however, is marked not by the advancement of time but by its recurring patterns. Cyclical time is, ironically, "timeless" because it is governed by the daily, weekly, monthly and annual cycles that exist in the natural world.

Cyclical time teaches us humility. For while we can act in historical time to advance ourselves and affect change, we cannot alter natural cycles of day to night, summer to fall and winter to spring. If historical time is empowering, cyclical time is humbling: it teaches us that something greater than our own efforts govern the universe. For many Jews, that "something" is called God.

Jewish tradition is remarkable in that it realizes that both cyclical and historical times are important and necessary. Historical time lets us take stock of our lives, evaluate our choices and determine what we want to change. Cyclical time helps us appreciate the recurring patterns of our lives and helps us balance our need for control, success and advancement with the wisdom that "to everything, there is a season."

I measure my own good fortune today by how wonderful it feels to have so many blessings in my life. I know that there will be times ahead when I will face personal challenges, struggle with family issues, and be confronted by problems for which I have no answer. But it is because of this knowledge, that things will and must change, that I am determined to stop the clock right now and offer a prayer of gratitude.

Everything You Always Wanted to Know about Sex...

I walked up to the podium and faced the crowd—a group of about fifty men in business suits who wanted nothing more than to finish the conference and head straight to the bar for Happy Hour.

This group is going to be tough to please, I thought as I noticed them pecking away on their BlackBerrys. The talk I had prepared on Jewish business ethics called "Putting God in your Briefcase" didn't seem like such a good idea anymore. So, like a ship heading into the wind, I quickly changed tack and set sail into new waters.

"I'd like to talk about something we're all interested in," I opened boldly. A few heads tipped back, eyes curious and waiting.

"Something that my mother told me you never bring up in mixed company," I continued blushing. I could see I had captured their interest.

"SEX!" I blurted into the microphone, amidst laughter and a few hoots.

"And Judaism," I added, causing more laughter. I was beginning to feel like I was writing a Woody Allen script.

"How many of you think that Judaism thinks that sex is bad?" I asked. More than half the hands in the room went up, and a wise guy retorted "Depends upon the girl."

"No, actually, it depends upon the man," I responded and watched as the audience collectively leaned forward to hear what I would say next.

In Judaism, sex is not considered shameful, sinful or obscene. It is a natural, physical desire born of the *yetzer hara*, the evil inclination. Despite its name, the evil inclination is not all bad, because without it, we would not have the drive to promote our own well-being or strive for personal achievement and success. In fact, the Talmud teaches that without the evil inclination, we would not build a house, marry, have children or conduct a business. To emphasize this point, the rabbis concluded that "the greater the man, the greater his evil inclination."

Jewish tradition teaches that sex is permissible only within the context of marriage. It is not merely a way of experiencing physical pleasure but is an act of immense significance, requiring commitment, responsibility and spiritual awareness. Sex unifies a couple, joining body and soul together, and brings them into a covenantal relationship mirroring the relationship between God and Israel.

In the Torah, the Hebrew word for sex is *da'at*, which means "to know." Jewish sexuality is defined as more than physical pleasure; it is an intimacy and spiritual awareness that encompasses both the heart and mind. But Judaism does not ignore the physical nature of sexuality. The need for physical compatibility between husband and wife is so important that Jewish law requires the couple to meet at least once before the wedding. If either finds the other physically objectionable, the marriage is not to take place.

Sex in a marriage is deemed a *mitzvah* when it is done to reinforce the bond between husband and wife. But in no event is sex ever to be performed out of spite or revenge, and any type of forced sexual relations are strictly prohibited under Jewish law.

What may come as a tremendous surprise to Jews who perceive Judaism as patriarchal and chauvinistic is that Jewish law has always treated sex as the woman's right, not the man's. A husband has a duty to sexually gratify his wife regularly and to ensure that sex is pleasurable for her. He is also obligated to watch for signs that his wife wants sex, and to offer it to her without her asking for it. These concepts are quite revolutionary considering that they evolved over two thousand years ago in the ancient Near East where women were treated as property and subservient to men.

Taking this liberated concept one step further, the Talmud prescribes the amount of sex that couples should have based on the man's occupation.

For a man of leisure (unemployed)—every day

For regular laborers—twice a week

For donkey drivers (who travel to nearby towns)— once a week

For camel drivers (who travel to distant places)— once a month

For Sailors—once every six months

For Torah scholars—Sabbath eve

Lest you think Judaism is only sensitive toward women, a wife does not have discretion to withhold sex from her husband as a form of punishment. If she does, he may divorce her without paying the divorce settlement provided for in the marriage contract (*Ketubah*).

I concluded my talk to a room filled with men who now knew more about the Jewish view of sex than Dr. Ruth and Dr. Laura combined. As I left the podium I overheard one man say to a friend: "Well that clinches it for me. My career as a camel driver is over!"

Rosh Hodesh: Finding Strength One Month at a Time

I listened to the phone message from Cindy and knew something was wrong. I could hear it in her voice, through the static on my answering machine. I called her back immediately and my heart sank as she spoke the words: "I have breast cancer."

From that day on, Cindy's world revolved around her cancer. Every decision, appointment, and choice, even the food she ate, related to her illness. We didn't speak often because she needed to conserve her energy, but when we did, she shared some of her ongoing concerns. How would she tolerate the next chemo session? Would she be too tired to attend her daughter's school play? Should she shave her head or wait for her hair to fall out? Would she ever feel normal again? So many questions with so few answers left Cindy feeling uncertain, scared and depressed. Even her doctor's assurance that she would feel better in eight months did little to cheer her.

Cindy tried to go to synagogue every Saturday; something she had done pre-cancer, but which now gave her the sense of normalcy that she so desperately needed. And it was there, sitting among friends at Shabbat morning services, that she discovered the true meaning and power of the *Rosh Hodesh* prayer, and a way to bring hope back into her life.

The Rosh Hodesh prayer is said at the beginning of each month when the new moon appears. Rosh Hodesh became a holiday of great significance in ancient times, before the Jewish lunar calendar was established. The new moon's sighting by at least two witnesses, together with the rabbinic court's declaration, signified the date upon which all other holidays were fixed. Fires on the hilltops of Jerusalem started a chain reaction from one community to the next, notifying Jewish settlements throughout Israel and the Diaspora that it was Rosh Hodesh. Sacrifices were offered, special prayers were chanted and festive meals were eaten—as the sound of the shofar echoed throughout the land.

Today we celebrate Rosh Hodesh once a month in synagogue, when we recite special blessings and prayers, beginning with: "May it be your will, Lord our God and God of our ancestors, to renew our lives in the coming month and bring us well-being and blessing."

Cindy had recited that prayer by rote many times before, but had never really considered its meaning. Those words became a touchstone for her and helped bring an order to the chaotic life that her cancer had created. They became a measuring rod for her progress: she just had to get through her treatments one month at a time until she had a chance to ask for another month of renewed health and blessings.

Living with cancer made Cindy more reflective,

aware and grateful of what it means to be alive. The Rosh Hodesh prayer gave her a time in which to speak to God and acknowledge her appreciation with these words: "Eternal God, Source of life, as a new month approaches, we are reminded of the passing of the seasons, of the preciousness of time, and of the limits of our earthly journey."

And now, many years later, she looks back at that difficult period of her life with renewed appreciation— for her body's strength, for the support of her friends and community and for the comfort and hope that the Rosh Hodesh prayer gave her each month. Its closing words are ones she strives to live by: "a life marked by true piety and the dread of sin; a life free from shame and reproach…a life filled with the love of Torah and reverence for God…."

Rosh Hodesh is more than a holiday. It's a monthly opportunity for spiritual renewal, a chance to look at our lives, one month at a time, and recognize that we have the continuing power to start over. It's also a time to realize that no matter how difficult our struggles may be, or how hard life is at this point in time, we only need to make it to another month, when we can ask again for renewed strength and blessings.

Witnessing Death:
A Lesson in Living

I sat beside her bed, watching her breathe. She looked so tiny, wrapped in mounds of bedcovers, her head softly resting on an oversized pillow. She no longer recognized me, or so I was told by her caregivers, but that didn't stop me from speaking continuously to her as I stroked her hairless head.

I placed a tape deck next to her bed and played all of her old favorites, trying to keep her connected to this world. Everyone who was part of the hospice team confirmed what I intuitively knew: that even in her unconscious state, she could hear the sounds around her and feel us as we stroked her arm or caressed her face. Sound and touch, two amazing senses, were what kept us tethered to each other now.

I loved my Aunt Gen, who was my "sometimes mother," but more often my friend and confidante. It was hard to believe that in days, perhaps hours, I would no longer be able to pick up the phone and call her for a quick chat, a bit of advice, or a family recipe my kids had come to love.

I had never witnessed death up close before, and

to be honest, I was terribly afraid. There were so many unknowns that I didn't want to even think about, let alone witness. How does death look? How does it sound? What if she is in pain? How can I help her be at peace after all of the months she fought so valiantly as a warrior against cancer?

Slowly, hour by hour, something began to happen to me. The more time I spent with Gen, quietly watching the changes in her body as her life ebbed away, the more I grew comfortable with my fears. And with the process of dying itself. I watched her like a new mother watching a sleeping infant—with wonder, amazement and awe. I studied her every change—a slight loss of color in her right hand, a pause or hiccup in her breathing, a fluttering behind her eyelids—each time realizing that this is what death looks like. I didn't realize then what I know now—that I was lucky to be able to view her death as a natural process. Like waves in an outgoing tide, her life force was drawn away from us as her body relinquished resistance and her soul found its way home.

Toward the end, I would get annoyed when visitors came and acted as if they knew what to do. "Turn up the music," a friend would counsel. "Try to make her eat," another would coach. Each person meant well, but only those of us who surrounded her daily could see that she no longer wanted to be drawn into the chaos of life. She had transitioned into a place of existence that no longer included us. What was hardest on me was the realization that, inevitably, we would all be left without her.

My thoughts during those final days were sharper

and more focused than I would have expected. All of
the errands that I had left undone and the work that
was piling up on my desk seemed irrelevant now. What
mattered most was being close, not just to Gen but to
those of us who loved and cared for her. Being, not doing,
was the only thing that seemed to make sense in that
time and space. And in those long hours of being, I experienced an intimacy with my family, within myself and
with God that I had never known before.

There is clarity of purpose that emerges when someone
we love is dying. It helps us focus on what is truly important in our life and let go of things that no longer serve
us. It makes us aware of the impermanence of our days
and that there is no time better than the present to say
the things we need to say to those we love. It forces us to
recognize that we, too, will die and inspires us to make
every day count.

Soon after Gen died, I felt an urgency to set things
right with a family member from whom I had grown
distant. Something had happened between us and we just
couldn't break through our discomfort. Gen's death not
only gave me permission, it acted as a mandate to speak
what was in my heart. The conversation we had not only
cleared things up between us but helped me see another
gift that Gen had given me. That it is not death which we
should fear, but a life not fully and honestly lived.

Living
with Integrity

That's Funny, You Don't Look *Jewish!*

That's funny, you don't look Jewish!" was a typical comment I heard as I was growing up. "The freckles and all make you look, oh, I don't know…Irish?"

I was never quite sure what the appropriate response to that remark should be. Was it a compliment to which I should say "Thank you" or an insult that might merit a sarcastic retort. What does it mean to "look Jewish," anyway? Was I not tall enough; was my hair too fine and straight? If there is a Jewish look, why didn't I get the right genes?

I grew up in a small town in New Jersey with a very small Jewish community. When my parents bought a home there in 1950, they were assured that everyone was very friendly to Jews and were taken to the local synagogue to alleivate any fears they might have had. But looking back, I don't think they could have predicted that I would be only one of a dozen Jewish kids in a high school class of 350. Nor could they have understood the responsibility that being in such a minority placed on my small shoulders.

In seventh grade I became the Defender of the Faith, a faith that I barely understood myself. At slumber parties, I would find myself explaining, often defensively, why I didn't eat bacon with my eggs, believe in Jesus or celebrate Christmas "like normal kids." In 9th grade at cheerleading tryouts, I was asked to spell my last name. I remember the coach's question to this day: "Hirshberg. Let's see. Is that U-R-G or E-R-G?" It didn't hit me until after I was picked for the squad, that she was trying to figure out if I was Jewish or not. And when I told her that I wouldn't be at a football game because it was Rosh Hashanah, I drew looks of disapproval from the coach as well as my fellow cheerleaders who saw my religious commitment as disrespectful to the team.

During my junior year of college I lived in Israel, and one of the first things I did when I arrived was head straight to a phone booth. I knew enough Hebrew to find it: My name, Hirshberg, showed up more than 30 times on those onion skin pages of the phonebook. I walked into the Jerusalem sun, beaming with pride. I was finally at home in a land where no one would ever think of asking me how I spelled my last name.

As a parent I have spent countless hours thinking about, talking about, and strategizing with my husband about what will make Judaism meaningful to our family, especially our children. Over the years we have repeatedly asked ourselves what we can do to ensure that our children's Jewish identity will be important to them as they leave home and enter college, relationships, marriage and careers.

But is there a formula, a "Jewish Identity Recipe" for us to follow? Is a summer at Camp Ramah enough to do the trick? What about Hebrew Day School or a family trip to Israel? Does having a Bar or Bat Mitzvah guarantee continued commitment? What if we have Friday night dinners together every week?

The answer to the question is that there is no single or simple answer to the question. In my case, being in a minority helped me develop a healthy sense of Jewish pride. With so few Jews around, it became important for me to learn more about what being Jewish meant so that I could explain, even defend it, to others.

As my mother would say about most of child-raising: "Half of it is hard work and the other half is *mazel*," or luck. A family can be committed to creating a warm Jewish home and have children who do not follow the same path. A child from a non-observant home can meet a Jewish teacher or camp counselor and be inspired to become engaged in Jewish life. Who we are, where we live, and the influences, both positive and negative, that affect our lives will ultimately shape the relationship that we have toward Judaism and our Jewish identity.

The one thing that is certain, however, is this: If, as parents, we model a life that is rich in Jewish values such as kindness, charity, compassion and respect for the rights of others; if we engage in positive relationships with other Jews in our community; and if we create meaningful rituals and traditions in our homes that bring our family closer, then there is a far greater chance that our children will want to do the same as they build a home and family of their own.

Did You Hear about the Goldmans?

They sat hunched over their coffee cups and bagels, like team members in a huddle. I tried to concentrate on the newspaper I was reading but their voices distracted me. They were talking about a good friend of mine, and before long, I had rearranged my body so that I could fully eavesdrop without straining my neck.

"Did you hear that they aren't even speaking to one other and that her children have refused to come home for the holidays?" I heard one woman ask.

"Well, I heard that her son dropped out of school, but drugs may be involved, so you can't blame it on the divorce," another retorted.

"He was always a problem kid. Every time my son spent time with him, there was trouble," came the final, biting response.

I got up and headed for the door, leaving my half-eaten bagel on the table and taking my discomfort over what I had heard with me.

It's no secret that life can be challenging: creating a good marriage and raising a healthy family are difficult and complex tasks. But the problems we face are often made worse when talked about unkindly by others. And while I admit that I, too, have gossiped at times, I also know first-hand how much it hurts to be the subject of hurtful talk.

The act of gossiping is nothing new. From the beginning of time, we have spoken poorly about others, which is why the Torah commands: "Do not go about as a talebearer among your fellows." (Leviticus 19:16)

Lashon hara, or "evil tongue" in Hebrew, is the making of derogatory remarks about a person that will lower his or her status in the eyes of others, even though the comments are true. Unlike the American laws of libel and slander, which prohibit the making of untrue statements about a third party, lashon hara goes even further, prohibiting statements that are true, but damaging nonetheless.

Through our words we have the power to create, communicate, enlighten, heal and love; we also have the power to impair, diminish, denigrate, humiliate and destroy. Yet most of us take more time in choosing the clothes we wear, the food we eat and the movies we watch than in choosing the words we use every day when speaking to or about our children, parents, co-workers, teachers and friends.

The rabbis of the Talmud compared gossip to murder because it kills three people: the person who says it, the person who listens to it and the person about whom it is said. Yet they also understood that there are times when it is necessary to speak candidly about others, even though it may damage their reputation. In matters of marriage, employment or business transactions, Jewish law permits us to communicate information that might adversely affect those decisions.

Gossip may be an inevitable part of being a member of the human family. But talking badly about others does more than just damage their reputation in the community. It damages our own. For when we speak negatively about others, we say as much about who we are and what we value as individuals as we do about the person of whom we are speaking.

A Blind Date That Opened My Eyes

When I was a sophomore in college, my mother insisted that I meet Philip, the "brilliant" son of a dear friend of hers. "He's bright, handsome and has a wonderful sense of humor!" she promised me in a tone I had come to disbelieve from past experience. Nevertheless, I reluctantly agreed to meet him in exchange for the use of our family car for a weekend camping trip I was dying to take with my friends. It seemed like a good deal—until a week later when the doorbell rang and in walked Phillip.

Phillip was hardly what you would call a "looker." He was shorter than I and looked through large, coke-bottle glasses that kept slipping off his nose. Even though I wasn't very picky, I confess that I did a double-take when he took off his hat. Phillip's premature balding took me totally by surprise.

I knew he was smart because he was in med school, but we spent half an hour driving in circles trying to find the restaurant he had chosen for dinner. And as for funny—the joke was on me, because we ended up at a Benny Hanna Steak House and I was a strict vegetarian.

The evening went from bad to worse but I tried

my best to smile my way through it. I answered "thank you" to almost every question he asked, including what I was majoring in at school. On the way home, I became a bit anxious about how to avoid the inevitable "good-night kiss." That's when I started sneezing and rubbing my nose, hoping that, as a med student, he would have a thing about germs and dump me at my door.

Just my luck, Philip saw my symptoms as a chance to do a little arm-chair diagnosing. According to him, I had sinusitis and an acute reaction to the cinnamon air freshener he had sprayed in his car before our date. But as he talked, my feelings softened as I felt his genuine concern. He was a decent guy and true to the gentleman he was, he walked me to the door and bowed a dignified good night.

Many years later I ran into Philip, today a well-known internist in New York City. Yes, he was bald, but so are most of the men I know, and his warmth and humor were contagious as we talked. We caught up on the past, laughing about our one and only disastrous date.

"I'm glad I ran into you," he said. "I've always wanted to thank you for something."

"Thank me, for what?" I thought sheepishly to myself. "For being such a jerk?"

"For pretending you had a good time with me the night I took you out. I had just finished a miserable year at school and was feeling pretty low about myself. You were nice, smiled a lot, and even though I knew you wouldn't go out with me again, you made me feel good. That helped me through some rough times."

We hugged and I felt genuine this time when I smiled and waved goodbye. It made me reflect on how little we understand the impact that our actions have on others, even those we know for only a short moment in our lives. Perhaps that is why our Jewish sages taught that when a person meets another with a cheerful countenance, even if he offers him nothing, he is credited with having given away one of the best gifts in the world. It may be true that we can never know the effect that our responses have on others, but we can be certain of one thing. No one has ever become poorer from the giving of a smile, a warm handshake or a few kind words.

Finding Pride and Identity in a Foreign Land

Brazil was nothing like I had expected it would be. For some reason, probably based on my ignorance more than anything else, I imagined myself amidst goats, cows and adobe huts in a third-world type of place, taking afternoon siestas in a hammock while drinking rum out of a coconut. The hammock and rum part were pretty accurate but my third-world assumptions couldn't have been farther from the truth.

My family's primary reason for going to Brazil was to see our daughter Lauren, who was living there as an exchange student at the time. Beyond just holding her and seeing that she was still in one piece, we really didn't care much what we did.

Our reunion was tearful and joyous and we couldn't stop marveling at how grown-up and self-assured our daughter had become. As we headed to the beach home where Lauren's Brazilian family lived during the summer, she talked non-stop about the country and her experiences, mixing Portuguese with English as she spoke. Despite the exhausting 20-hour trip, I soaked up images of sugar cane fields, rolling hills and tiny towns as I savored the fresh cashews and ice-cold coconut water we bought from a roadside fruit stand. As we approached the city of Joa Pessoa, the sea coast opened up and a skyline filled with colorful buildings lay before us.

Brazil is a huge country, slightly smaller than the United States, with regions that vary from desert to mountainous to tropical. Its spectacular 4,655 miles of Atlantic coastline is the home of numerous coastal cities where modern buildings stand adjacent to colonial forts and churches. And everywhere you go, there is music, people and chatter in the streets, although nobody we heard spoke English.

Almost 75 percent of Brazil's 186 million residents are Catholic. When Lauren first decided to go, this caused me some concern because I knew that she would have little opportunity to connect with Jews for an entire year. Not to mention all those good-looking Brazilian boys who would no doubt be a part of the picture! But I was not prepared for the fact that once she got to Campina Grande, where she lived during the school year, there would not be a single Jewish person in that city of 350,000 people. Or that no one she met, from her large, extended Brazilian family to her classmates and friends, had ever met a Jew before.

Any normal Jewish mother would probably have begun looking for flights from Rio de Janeiro to Tel Aviv at this point, but I just held my breath and trusted that whatever was meant to happen, would happen. After all, we Jews have lived in the Diaspora for more than 2,000 years and have been amazingly successful in preserving our faith, rituals and community in "foreign" lands. But the question lingered: Would my 18-year-old daughter be able to do the same?

The answer came toward the end of her first month, when she called and asked if I would send her a "Shabbat box" so she could light candles on Friday night. What she missed most, she confided, was our family connection— lighting candles and sharing Shabbat dinner as a family.

As Rosh Hashanah approached, she started to search for a synagogue to go to for the holidays, which had become even more important to her now that she had so little opportunity to be with other Jews. With a great deal of effort she found one in Recife, a city more than two hours away, and a Jewish family to host her for the holidays. In a town she had never been to, in a country 10,000 miles from home, Lauren sat in the women's section of the Sephardic synagogue next to the Rabbi's wife and prayed in Hebrew while our family said the same prayers in Tucson.

But what really moved me was when Lauren called and asked for my latke recipe. We had sent her a "Cha-nukkah box"—complete with menorah, candles, *dreidels* and *gelt* so that she could celebrate the holiday. But she had other ideas. In addition to celebrating each night by herself, she was determined to share her holiday with her new family and friends, to teach them about the Macabees and the re-dedication of the Temple in Jeru-salem. And, of course, to treat them to delicious potato latkes and home-made applesauce, which, without a grater, took the entire day to make!

Like most parents, I often wonder (and angst over) whether the ideals, values and family traditions that we have tried to instill in our children will be important to them as they mature into adults. I know first-hand how difficult and painful it is to let our children go their own ways. But I also know that the choices they make and the paths they follow will lead them to better understand who they are and what is most important to them. If we have given them the tools, we have to have faith that they will find their own way to have a meaningful relationship with Judaism and with God.

If a Tree Falls in the Forest, What Do You Hear?

When I was a little girl, I used to take long walks with my dad in our neighborhood. Sometimes he would tie pieces of candy to the branch of a tree before our walk, which I would delight in finding when he pointed to a bird or colorful leaves. I believed in magic, I believed in the power of trees and I believed him when he told me that the "GF" (Good Fairy) had left them for me. It wasn't until I grew up that I realized that GF actually stood for Good Father.

On one such walk Dad presented me with my first riddle: "If a tree falls in the forest and no one is there to hear it, does it makes a sound?"

I didn't know the answer then, and am not certain I do to this day. But I am as grateful for the curiosity he inspired in me as I was for the pocket full of lifesavers I savored at the time.

Jewish tradition has its own variation of the tree riddle. Nearly 2,000 years ago, Rabbi Eliezer taught that: "In the hour when you cut down a tree which bears fruit, its voice goes out from one end of the universe to the other, yet its voice is not heard."

This powerful image, of the silent scream of a felled tree heard throughout the world, is an indication of how important trees, and all of nature are, in the Jewish tradition.

Trees hold a place of honor in Jewish texts, the Jewish calendar and the Jewish spirit. The Torah tells us that "man is like the tree of the field" and commands us not to destroy any fruit trees (*Bal taschit*) in the midst of taking the spoils of war. We celebrate the New Year for the trees on *Tu B'Shvat* and plant trees for our children when they are born. We call the Torah *Atz Chaim*, the Tree of Life, because it provides us with spiritual sustenance, much as trees provide us with physical nourishment. And we are taught: "If while holding a sapling in your hand you are told that the Messiah is about to arrive, first plant the sapling and then go out to receive the Messiah."

It is the second part of Rabbi Eliezer's image, however, of the wailing voice of the tree no one hears, that sends chills down my spine. The rabbis wrote about the issues of their day, attempting to unravel the mysteries of life and make sense of their problems. Could it be that 2,000 years ago, they were concerned that a society that had lost its sensitivity to the destruction of trees would lose its ability to care for each other?

You don't have to look far to see or hear the consequences of the natural world screaming back at us today. Regardless of partisan affiliations, we can't deny the emerging evidence of the negative effects that global warming is having on the world community. Our warmer climate is heating up ocean waters, fuelling hurricanes and tsunamis. The current drought in the Amazon, the melting glaciers, the rising water levels are all suspected to be the result of rising ocean temperatures. The list is long and getting longer and everything is interconnected, endangering not just thousands of animal and plant species but the human species as well.

There are things all of us can do, as concerned members of the Jewish community and as citizens of the world community. *Bal taschit* tells us not to destroy our environment: it requires us to consciously manage our resources and avoid waste wherever possible. Using environmentally friendly building products in our homes and offices, recycling waste products, reducing our energy demands by using compact fluorescent lights, lowering our thermostats, replacing our air filters, using less fuel and buying more fuel efficient cars are just a few of the things we can do that will, collectively, make a difference. If we have learned one thing from Jewish history, it is this: it's the collective efforts of each one of us that ensures the future for us all.

If we ask ourselves the tree riddle today, perhaps it should be this: If a tree falls in the forest, what will we hear and what will we do about it? *Bal Taschit* is the first step in answering the question.

Questioning As
an Act of Faith

Are You There, God? It's Me, Amy

In 1997, my family and I moved to Jerusalem where I participated in a year-long program at Hebrew University with a group of international Jewish educators. We had a magical year together; one that permitted us to become totally engrossed in living, learning, eating, praying and absorbing everything we could about Israel and our Jewish faith. As a student, I spent many hours in classrooms on the Mt. Scopus campus, but one of the most significant memories I have of learning that year was not at the university. It was at Kol HaNeshama, a wonderful synagogue within walking distance of our apartment, where every Monday morning my husband and I took a class together in Jewish prayer from Rabbi Levi Kelman.

One week, a friend of ours, Rabbi Elie Kaplan-Spitz, taught the class. He spoke about the history and development of prayer: how it originated from animal and agricultural sacrifices which Aaron, and then later his descendants, officiated at daily. And that when the Jewish people entered the land of Israel, sacrificial altars were set up until eventually sacrifice was centralized in the Holy Temple in Jerusalem.

When the First Temple was destroyed in 586 B.C.E., prayers with words were developed to substitute for sacrifices so that the Jews in exile could have a way to communicate with God. When the Temple was rebuilt 50 years later, sacrifice was reinstituted until the destruction of the Second Temple in 70 C.E. Since then, prayers have taken the place of sacrifice, synagogues have replaced the Holy Temple and rabbi-scholars act in the role of the Temple priests.

During class that day, we were given an assignment. We were asked to write a letter to God (or whatever we called the Higher Power in our lives) as if we were friends. And for the next 15 minutes, that is what we did.

I was a little nervous at first and somewhat self-conscious. How DO you write a letter to God? What do you say? What kind of language do you use? Do you tell God about a problem, or share something fun that you did or let him know about a great shoe sale at the mall? After the first few paragraphs it became much easier, and I was amazed at how much fun I had as the words began to flow more naturally.

I thought the assignment was finished, and was quite pleased with myself until Elie turned to us and said: "Now that you have written your letter to God, I want you to write a letter back to yourself as if you are God."

Whoa! That was a little farther than I had planned to go. How could I do that? What kind of audacity did he think I had to respond to myself as if I were God? I picked up my pen, drawing circles on my paper, unsure of how or where to start. I looked over at my husband Ray who was doing the same thing

But then, I did the unthinkable. I began to write back to myself as if I were God. The words I wrote to myself came from a place of love: they were words of understanding, encouragement, hope and forgiveness; not words of chastisement, guilt or shame. I wrote and wrote and wrote, tears spilling onto the pages next to my words. When I finished I was exhausted and more than a bit shaky. But it felt exhilarating to have spent this type of private time being so close to the Power that I call God.

The Temple priests and Jewish sages understood the power of being in relationship with God. The Hebrew word for sacrifice, *korban*, comes from the word *karov*, which means "to draw close." While we do not sacrifice today, we can let our prayers help us feel closer to God, even though we may be uncertain to whom we are speaking or how to say it.

The next time you are in synagogue and get bored or are distracted by other thoughts, try to think about what prayer is really meant to be and do—a pathway to connect you to the Divine through which your innermost thoughts can be spoken and heard.

Does It Matter How I Pray?

I remember it as if it were yesterday. My beautiful 16-year-old daughter, dancing just the night before, lay motionless in the hospital bed in pain. She had fallen from the roof and shattered her third and fourth vertebrae.

Her father and I privately nursed our worst fears about what lay ahead: from permanent paralysis to a lifetime of chronic pain. My daughter was more upset about the immediate future. Would she have to miss her prom? Could she still perform in the school musical that was opening in two weeks? Would she be able to go back to school to finish her sophomore year?

The decision we had to make within the next eight hours was not an easy one: whether to have extensive surgery to fuse her broken back or rely upon a full body brace for six months in the hopes that it would heal properly. Both had risks and both had complications. She looked at her dad and me as if we had the answer. My mind was a blank with the exception of a simple line that kept repeating itself, over and over again: "Dear God, please let Lauren be okay."

Lauren broke my internal reverie with her own sweet voice.

"I want the surgery," she said, "so that I'll know for sure that my bones will heal in place."

Then she added, as if reading my mind, "I'm going to be okay, Mom."

Thankfully, those days are now a blur of doctors and medical decisions, of family and friends whose kindness filled our home with love, consolation and of course, food. For months afterward, I went to bed and woke up each morning with the same words running through my mind. "Dear God, please let her heal."

Praying to God in this way was not new to me because I have been in an ongoing conversation with God since I was a little girl. But my daily prayers caused me to wonder: Does it matter how I pray to God? Do my own heartfelt words have the same impact and effect as traditional Jewish prayer?

Prayers from the heart have always been recognized as authentic in the Jewish tradition. The Torah is replete with examples of unique and personal prayers, most often offered in the context of an immediate need or request for protection, guidance or healing. David petitioned God for refuge from Saul saying: "Hear my cry, O God; Attend unto my prayer." (Psalms 61:1) Moses pleaded with God to save his sister Miriam from leprosy by crying out: "Oh Lord, please heal her!" (Numbers 12:13) And Hannah, a barren woman who desperately wanted a son, prayed to God vowing, "then I shall give him to You (God) all the days of his life..." (Samuel I: 1:11)

From the beginning of time, we have used prayer as a vehicle to be in a relationship with God. It is the language of encounter, even when we are uncertain to whom we are speaking or what we want to say. Yet, traditional Jewish prayers have often been hard for me to relate to. The wording is stiff and archaic and the images do not speak to me personally. What has become clear to me, however, is the value of having precise and definite texts when praying together as a community.

When we pray together in community, we do much more than simply recite ancient Jewish texts: We affirm and honor our relationship to our ancestors. We speak for those who cannot speak for themselves and we offer comfort and support to those who don't have the strength. We affirm our history, tradition and peoplehood as we share the same liturgy with Jews the world over. And regardless of whether we pray in France, China or San Diego, our communal voice is always stronger than any individual voice alone.

Prayers from the heart have a place in the Jewish tradition alongside the ancient masterpieces of traditional communal expression. When we pray from a place of deep and personal direction, we pray with *kavannah* (which means "intentionality" in Hebrew). When we recite set liturgical prayers at specific times of day, we pray with *keva* (which means "fixed"). Neither is complete without the other. To be a part of the historical Jewish community, we pray with keva. To be in a unique and personal relationship with God, we pray with kavannah. Each way gives us opportunities to express our faith, desires, needs, gratitude, fears and hopes.

As our sages so wisely counseled us: "Hence, the Holy One declared to Israel: When you pray, pray in the synagogue in your city; if you cannot pray in the synagogue in your city, pray in your open field; if you cannot pray in your open field, pray in your house; if you cannot pray in your house, pray on your bed; if you cannot pray aloud on your bed, commune with your heart." (Midrash Tehilim 4:9)

Am I a "Bad" Jew?

Steven was only 10 years old the first time he was attacked for being a Jew. No, he wasn't called a "dirty Jew," "kike" or "Christ-killer" by some taunting bully or Anti-Semitic neighbor. His assault came from the inside, from a fellow student at the Hebrew day school he attended.

"You're hardly Jewish, you know. You don't keep kosher and you never go to synagogue," Benny scorned. "You're a *bad* Jew."

A bad Jew. To even the most assimilated Jew, the accusation cuts to the core. For while most of us can tolerate a wide variety of character assaults, to be accused of being a bad Jew feels different and much worse.

Why is it that within the Jewish religion, which encompasses a broad spectrum of ideas, rituals, traditions, foods and cultures, we are so quick to judge one another from the standpoint of where we are in our own relationship to Judaism? At the tender age of 11, Benny had already begun to negatively view Steven because he didn't follow the same observances that Benny's family did. Is it simply human nature to judge others based on our own choices or do we really believe that we are better Jews (and better people) because of the rituals we observe, the synagogues we attend, the committees we serve on and the charities we support?

Put another way, does the fact that I keep kosher make my cousin a bad Jew because he enjoys an occasional cheeseburger? Am I better Jew than my friend Ellen because I give to the Jewish Federation but she donates to the American Diabetes Foundation? I agree it makes us different Jews, but not necessarily better or worse.

I may be going out on a limb but I think that, as serious Jews, we need to ask ourselves these questions. Shouldn't the focus of our inquiry be whether we are engaged Jews, evolving Jews, questioning Jews and caring Jews rather than whether we are 'as good as the Goldberg family' Jews? Shouldn't we look at ourselves and ask ourselves how the Jewish tradition can provide a framework for meaning and purpose and enrich and inform our lives and families?

Being a Jew is a lifelong process. From the moment a Jewish baby enters the world, he or she does so with a different set of parents, genes, traditions, opportunities, challenges, expectations and responsibilities. Judaism teaches us that each one of us is unique. From this we understand that each one of us will encounter and embrace the Torah and its ideals in ways that are unique to us.

What that means for each person will inevitably be different. For some it may mean engaging in Torah study and ritual observance. For others it may mean going to

Israel, buying Israeli bonds or supporting the Community Food Bank. For still others it may mean being involved in creating a Jewish home and family, joining a synagogue, participating in social action programs or working out at the Jewish Community Center.

The fact that the point of entry for everyone is different matters little as long as the pursuit in some way enhances our awareness and appreciation of Jewish traditions, ethics, history and people. The Hebrew term for Jewish law is *Halakah*, which means "path" or "way." We do ourselves and other Jews an injustice if we fail to acknowledge that walking along the Jewish path is an evolving, fluid process, with each new awareness, decision and understanding informing and guiding our future as we engage in our own very unique way of Jewish living.

Respect and love for one another, not just as human beings but as Jewish human beings, is derived from our ability to recognize and value not just the similarities between us but the differences as well.

A favorite saying of the rabbis of Yavneh was:

"I am a creature of God and my neighbor is also a creature of God.
I work in the city and he works in the country.
I rise early for my work and he rises early for his work.
Just as he cannot excel in my work, I cannot excel in his work.

Will you say that I do great things and he does small
things?

We have learned that it does not matter whether a
person does much or little, as long as he directs
his heart to heaven."

Babylonian Talmud, Brachot, 17a

When asked if he put on *tefillin* each morning, noted
German Jewish scholar and author Franz Rosenzweig
responded "Not yet." While he may not have been ready
to commit to doing it at that point in time, he didn't
close the door on the possibility that someday he might
be. What a wonderful way to envision the potential that
remains open to each of us as we journey into new ter-
ritories of being Jewish.

Why the Holocaust
Will Never Be Forgotten

I did not recognize the woman's voice on my answering machine, with its thick European accent and apologetic tone. Nor did I relate the fact that I was teaching a course on Holocaust literature to her call. But once I met Gabrielle, I knew it was more than chance that caused her to ask me to help her publish a book she had written about her life.

I'll admit that at first I was reluctant to call her back. I was over my head in work and was leaving for a trip in a few days. But I left her message on my machine and replayed it several times throughout the day. Something about her voice haunted me and for reasons that I still don't understand, I knew that returning her call would change my life. And I was right, because it did.

From the first time I met her, she captured my heart. I stood on her doorstep and watched through the window as Gabrielle, barely five feet tall and burdened by arthritis and numerous aches and pains, struggled to get out of her chair to greet me. We walked into her dining area where the table was set with a plate of cookies, some mineral water, and a box of candies. I sat across from her, her face framed by her artwork on the wall behind her—paintings that expressed the darkest days of her life.

She was animated one minute, telling me about when she first met Mr. Schneider, her husband of 40 years, and pensive the next, her eyes resting on the photo of her sister Sydonia, whom she held in her lap as she lay dying in Bergen-Belsen. And when she reminisced about her childhood, before the Nazi's destroyed it, there was coyness in the way she held her head and a girlish blush colored her cheeks.

Since our first visit, Gabrielle has drawn me into her world. She is physically limited and can no longer move about easily but that doesn't stop her from getting what she needs. Her strength comes from years of being willful and determined against the most impossible of odds. But her generosity of spirit—that is what touches me most. She has lived through years of extreme deprivation, losing so much when she was so young, but she is generous, loving and giving to a fault. I have never left her house without her handing me something special or beautiful as a keepsake.

I look at her wide-open face and a line from *The History of Love* comes back to me. "Show me a Jew that survives and I'll show you a magician." Throughout her 83 years, Gabrielle has worked her magic on those around her. I am convinced that is why she survived and why she couldn't rest until her story was told.

For many years after the war, few people in Israel spoke or wrote about the Nazi atrocities, forcing survivors to cope with their nightmares in silence. One person who understood the significance of survivors telling their stories was David Ben Gurion, who knew that in order for his fledgling country to begin to heal, survivors had to speak out. For this reason, he decided in 1962 to televise the trial of Adolph Eichmann, the first televised trial in history. For four grueling months, hundreds of survivors relived their nightmares while the world watched in horror and disbelief.

Since that time, hundreds of personal stories, memoirs, novels and films have been brought to the world's attention. After filming Schindler's List, Steven Spielberg established "Survivors of the Shoah Visual History" to document the stories and experiences of survivors and witnesses to make certain they were never lost. Today over 52,000 testimonies in 32 different languages from people in 56 countries fill these archives. Gabrielle's story is one of them.

But she has taken it one step further: She has written and self-published a book of stories, together with her paintings, entitled *Andor Kept His Promise from the Grave.* It is the testimony of a life lived with courage, humor, inspiration and love told by a woman who has survived humanity's darkest hours but has never stopped believing in the goodness of people.

When Gabrielle first called me about her book, I assumed I would have a few limited conversations with her about the publishing world and that would be it. But I have gained more from our time together than I ever could have imagined. Her stories, struggles and courage have inspired me to reflect on my own life and choices and have given me the perspective I sometimes lack.

And now I understand clearly why Gabrielle had to write her book: She did it in order to make sense of why she survived when so many others did not.

"I had a duty" she told me with tears in her eyes, "because I was the one who survived." And I am so grateful she did.

Multiple Faiths, One Simple Prayer

I'd be lying if I told you it was an ordinary day. The gathering of almost 100 people opened to the beating of the drums of the Panther Creek Intertribal Drummers followed by a blessing from the Elders from the Old Pasqua Village. The crowd intuitively swayed together as we tried to embrace peace and wisdom from the four corners of the Earth.

The hair on my arms stood straight up, a visceral acknowledgement of the spiritual energy that literally charged the room. On the dais sat a multi-faith panel of clergy: a Jewish Rabbi, a Catholic Bishop, a Methodist Reverend, a Muslim Imam and His Holiness, the Dalai Lama, each of whom were asked to share the essence of their faiths.

I sat on the edge of my chair, soaking in their words and hoping that I was worthy of this sacred moment. I could barely hold the pen in my hand so I abandoned any idea of taking detailed notes. Thankfully, the journalist in me kept scribbling comments on the back of the program, which is the only reason I can remember now what I learned that morning while in a half-trance.

As each person spoke, it became clear that regardless

of what words were used to describe God or different religious traditions and beliefs, each faith was built on the same foundations—that of love, compassion, tolerance, forgiveness and self-discipline. And, at the heart of each faith was the belief that peace is the essence of true understanding, justice and truth.

In Judaism, the meaning of peace goes far beyond that of the absence of conflict. It is a state of being, of knowing and of living. Our sages said: "The world rests on three things—"Upon justice, upon truth and upon peace." And the three of them are intertwined: Where justice is done, truth comes into being and the purpose of justice and truth is to bring about peace.

The Dalai Lama said something that morning that was so simple and obvious that I was surprised that it felt like an epiphany to me: If we accept the idea that God is inconceivable and beyond human comprehension, then how can we possibly think that any two people, let alone any two religions, will ever agree about what God is or is not? And, he suggested, rather than trying to relate to each other based on our differing views of God, why not concentrate on the many values that our traditions share, such as love, compassion and forgiveness? This is the path, he concluded, that will lead to universal peace.

The morning ended with communal chanting; the blending of different hearts, minds, beliefs and faiths filling the room with a sound unlike any I had ever heard before. Our individual prayers and mantras converged as we joined hands and sang in unison: "Toward the One, United with All." I let myself imagine a time when we will all share a commitment to bring peace into the world through the values that unite us. I must have muttered my simple prayer aloud, for as I turned to leave, the woman sitting next to me smiled and said "Amen."

Celebrating the Joys, Not the Oys!

Rosh Hashanah: Is Your Spiritual Portfolio in Balance?

I grew up in a home where money was talked about openly and often. Not about how much money my dad made or about what other people earned, but about how to invest the money we had so that it would grow for our future.

"Most people make money with their hands, but if you're smart, you'll learn how to make money with you head," Dad would counsel me over chicken and green beans. And so, unlike other girls my age, I knew as much about stocks, bonds and price/earning ratios as I did about lip gloss, cheerleading and the Beatles. The net result was that I have invested in the stock market since the time I received my first paycheck.

Looking at my portfolio, especially before the Jewish High Holidays, reminds me of something that my father and I never discussed when I was young—whether my spiritual life is in order. Why the connection?

Because during the Jewish month of *Elul*, which occurs during the 30 days preceding Rosh Hashanah, we are challenged, as Jews, to evaluate our inner life and our outer commitments. This is the time of year when we take a hard look at our relationships, our obligations, our successes and our failings—to honestly assess if our "spiritual portfolio" needs to be rebalanced.

At Rosh Hashanah, we are required to ask ourselves questions like: What am I doing with my life? Am I satisfied with my goals, relationships and commitments? Do I give enough of myself? Where am I in my relationship with God? What do I want to change in the coming year? Can I be a better person, a more compassionate friend, a more caring daughter, a more supportive spouse? This type of hard questioning is called a *heshbon nefesh*, which in Hebrew literally means "an accounting of the soul."

In financial matters, it takes knowledge, discipline and personal awareness to properly manage a portfolio. These are the identical qualities needed to balance our "spiritual portfolios."

We must seek out knowledge—about Jewish living and Jewish literacy from the many Jewish resources that surround us including our teachers, rabbis, family, friends and community. We need discipline—to monitor ourselves and make choices that will further our personal and spiritual goals, promises and commitments. And we must cultivate our personal awareness—of who we are today, who we want to become and what support we may need from family and community to move forward on our journey.

We are each unique in our efforts to renew our spiritual lives. As with investing, each person begins with a different degree of confidence, a different knowledge base, and different fears or aversions. Yet Rosh Hashanah levels the spiritual playing field in that it gives each one of us an annual opportunity to engage in meaningful questioning and introspection which can lead to personal renewal and spiritual rebalancing. It is a beautiful reminder that we can always renew our commitment to live life with intention and purpose.

Sukkoth: Coming Together
under One Roof

The holiday of Sukkoth (which means "booths" in Hebrew) was not a big one on the Holiday Hit Parade in the town where I grew up. I did not know that it marked the season of harvest for Jews in ancient times or that it was the third pilgrimage festival after Passover and Shavuot. Not one single person I knew built a Sukkah in their back yard, so when my own son came home from our synagogue preschool and asked if we could have one, my initial response was less than enthusiastic.

"Why don't we just go and pick pumpkins instead?" I asked, hoping that Halloween might be a bigger draw.

"I want a Sukkah!" Josh responded with gusto. "We can eat in it every night and sleep in it, too. It's a *mitzvah*," he concluded, as if he knew that would clinch the deal.

And so, we dragged palm fronds from the alleyway and built a small lean-to in the back yard with sheets nailed on to three sides. It wasn't fancy, but it was a Sukkah in every sense of the word. A fragile, temporary structure that a strong wind could have destroyed, our first Sukkah withstood the weight of my children's expectations as well as that of the numerous gourds and ears of dried corn that we hung from its thatched roof.

As the years passed and my family's commitment to Jewish tradition grew, so did the size, shape and durability of our Sukkah. I will never forget the proud look on my husband's face the year we lived in Jerusalem and he built a sukkah the size of my first apartment (and decorated in much better taste!) Strings of bright colored lights and paper mache pineapples, strawberries and apples dangled over our heads as we dined with our friends for seven glorious nights.

Sukkoth is the start of the rainy season in Israel and prayers for bountiful rain, called *Hoshanot*, are recited every day of the holiday. It must work, because the very first night of Sukkoth, the sky unleashed a storm so great that it caused the reds and yellows of our paper fruits to bleed onto our T-shirts and chairs in a colorful pattern that no amount of bleach would remove.

As Jews, we are commanded to dwell in the Sukkah and to "take the fruit of the citron tree (etrog), the branches of date palms, twigs of a braided tree (myrtle), and willows of the brook (combined to make the lulav), and rejoice before the Lord for seven days." (Leviticus 23:40–43.)

We are further commanded to take these four species and shake them while reciting certain blessings. But why these four items rather than an orange, banana or peanuts? We find answers in Jewish *midrash*, interpretations of Biblical passages. One such midrash views these four items as symbolic of parts of our body. The etrog is our heart, the willow is our mouth, the myrtle represents our eye and the date palm branch is our backbone. The idea is that we can reach our highest potential as humans and honor God best when we bring our heart, mind and body to the task, just as the four species are brought together during the holiday of Sukkoth.

My favorite midrash suggests that the four species represent four types of Jews, each one in a different relationship with his or her faith and commitment to Torah. Some Jews are knowledgeable but do not act in ways that reflect Jewish values like compassion and justice. Others may lead with their hearts but have no formal Jewish training. Some may "feel Jewish" but not know how or where to begin to become connected to their Jewish roots. And others may have both the knowledge and the commitment to live their lives according to Jewish laws and values, becoming our role models and inspiration.

Sukkoth is an annual reminder that each one of us is unique and different but that together, we form the Jewish people. We all begin at different starting points; we encounter different challenges and are blessed with different strengths. We live in different cities and countries, we have different family compositions and we encounter the world with different eyes, hearts and minds. When we dine together in the Sukkah, we are called upon to create a time and place to honor these differences. For only when we are able to bring all Jews together under one roof, will we be able to reach our highest potential as human beings and as Jews.

Fighting Destruction and Violence: A Chanukah Commitment

I did something this week that I haven't done in a long time. And while what I did was not a crime, it made me feel like committing one by the end of the day. I spent the afternoon shopping for Chanukah gifts at the mall.

I started out feeling calm and confident that I could whip through the stores in a few hours and snatch up the perfect presents for all my little loved ones. But within 10 minutes, my confidence turned to frustration, then anger, as I walked through aisle after aisle of games like Mortal Kombat, Devil's Destruction and Ultra Violent World. I was particularly "inspired" by Grand Theft Auto which encourages children to use handguns, grenades, assault rifles, submachine guns and rocket launchers to hijack cars, demolish property and kill policeman just for the sport of it.

Call me old-fashioned, but isn't something terribly wrong with our culture when our best-selling toys encourage and even glorify aggression, destruction and violence? Shouldn't we try harder to deliver a more hopeful message to our children and grandchildren in this fragile and chaotic world?

I am certainly not the first to ask these questions. Ample scientific research indicates that toys and games that promote aggression and violence harm the development and behavior of children. The studies conclude that a direct correlation exists between children who play violent video and computer games and poor school performance, belligerence and physical fighting.

Going back more than two thousand years, "Jewish research" came to a similar conclusion about the effect of violence and destruction on the human psyche. In times of warfare, the Torah forbids us to destroy any fruit bearing-trees when we conquer a city. (Deuteronomy 20:19) We are commanded not to let our ego and our relationship to the world become distorted by our physical conquest of it. The significance of this idea is profound: In the midst of taking the spoils of war, we are required to maintain respect and regard for the earth.

Talmudic rabbis expanded this ban against destruction (called *bal tashchit* in Hebrew) to include a prohibition against tearing garments, destroying buildings, breaking vessels, clogging wells, diverting water, killing animals for convenience, wasting fuel and eating extravagant foods instead of simpler ones. Why so many additional restrictions? Because the rabbis understood a great deal about human nature: they realized that we do not easily set limits on ourselves and must be taught and trained NOT to be destructive.

Bal Tashchit teaches us not to destroy because destruction leads to more destruction. When we consciously refrain from destroying our habitat, when we preserve rather than waste our precious resources, when we maintain rather than damage our material possessions, we turn away from the negative within us and move toward the good. In seeking to preserve rather than destroy the world around us, we fulfill the Divine purpose for which we were created—to tend and care for the earth. (Genesis 2:15)

While the Talmudic rabbis did not contend with games like Mortal Kombat or Devil's Destruction, they understood the negative influence of destruction and sought to curtail it. Wouldn't it be wise this Chanukah if instead of buying our children toys that promote violence, we buy ones that promote peace, harmony and collaboration? Games like "Peace Games" which promotes positive, peaceful relationships through community service and social action or "In the Orchard," which encourages children to work together for a common goal. The internet is a good place to start for ideas and resources for similar games.

Mahatma Gandhi said it best when he said: "If we are to reach real peace in this world... we shall have to start with the children." Let's give peace a chance this Chanukah by choosing toys and games that reflect this commitment.

Passover and Bobby McGee

In the summer of 1968, just before I entered the ninth grade, I finagled my mother into driving over two hours to Atlantic City to take me and my best friend Cheryl to our very first rock concert. As we fled from the car to make sure that none of the cute older boys saw who the chauffeur was, our path was lit by the marquee with the name "Janis Joplin" emblazoned in yellow and orange lights.

Cheryl and I pretended to be nonchalant about being at the concert until Janis opened with "Me and Bobby McGee." From there on in, I screamed my way through the show, much to the chagrin of the college kids who were toking up a storm behind me. My mother fussed about how late it was as she drove us home, but joined in as we sang late into the night the one verse we knew by heart: "Freedom's just another word for nothing left to lose."

That line has resurfaced in my life repeatedly as a sort of mantra, especially when I was younger and things didn't work out the way I had planned. During times when I had no job, no boyfriend, or not much money, I was calmed by the thought that what I really had was "freedom." Freedom to do whatever I wanted, however I wanted, with whomever I wanted. Yeah, right!

Over the years, I have come to view freedom as something entirely different than the "nothing left to lose" concept of my youth. I now understand that freedom is quite the opposite of having no responsibility or ties. Genuine freedom comes with a large price tag because at the heart of freedom is free choice; the personal autonomy to exercise our will in the decisions we make in life.

The concept of freedom is essential to being human and being Jewish. It is what enables each of us, despite heredity, social conditions, and environment, to choose to do good or evil. If we did not have free will, then it would make little sense to have a book like the Torah, which is our guide on how to act and live. We are free—to follow its laws or not to follow its laws—but the choice is ours. The freedom we have to decide, to elect to seek goodness, justice and mercy over evil, injustice and intolerance is what makes the choice significant and meaningful.

It is fascinating to note that there are three distinct words in Hebrew for freedom. *Hofesh* refers to physical freedom, such as a vacation from work. *Dror* is the name of a bird and, like a bird that soars and migrates, it refers to mental freedom. *Cherut* describes the kind of freedom we have to pursue a higher purpose in life: it signifies spiritual freedom.

Passover is the Jewish holiday that commemorates our freedom from Egyptian bondage. The Hebrews who fled Egypt in the middle of the night had been slaves for over 400 years. Moses led them to physical freedom but it would take another 40 years of wandering in the Sinai desert before they would be able to relinquish their slave mentality and become free-thinking men and women. What would enable them to make this difficult transition?

The answer came seven weeks after the Exodus from Egypt at the foot of Mount Sinai, where the Hebrew people gathered to experience the most profound moment in Jewish history, the Revelation of the Torah. It was here that the people became unified as a *spiritual* nation, when they entered into the covenant with the God that brought them out of Egypt "with a strong hand and an outstretched arm." They were given freedom for a distinct and special purpose—to love God, to follow the laws of the Torah and to become a "kingdom of priests and a holy nation."

Passover is *Ziman Cherutanu*, which in Hebrew means the "time of our spiritual freedom." It is intricately linked to Shavuot, the holiday in which we celebrate the giving of the Torah. The journey of the Jewish people from redemption to Revelation is also the story of our redemption through Revelation. We are given our freedom so that we can become a holy people with a unique spiritual destiny.

This year, when we sit together at the Seder table and read the story of the Exodus from Egypt, let us remember that it is only because we are free, physically, mentally and spiritually, that we have the privilege of choosing how to live. And because of that freedom, we are never free from our responsibility to choose what is good and just.

But Mom, I Don't Want
a Bar Mitzvah!

I saw the blinking light on my answering machine and listened to the frantic voice of my girlfriend, Debbie, as I put the groceries away.

"Heeeeeelp! Jason says he doesn't want to do his Bar Mitzvah anymore. We've got the date and the place, I've hired the D.J. and he's already begun to prepare. He's making me crazy. What should I do? Call me."

Wow, what a bummer, I thought to myself.

But I really wasn't sure what to say in response to Debbie's S.O.S. What would I have done if my son had said, "No, thanks, Mom. I just don't want one." Or my daughter had decided she really didn't want the pressure and would rather wait until she was older.

Would I have forced them to do it anyway, because I knew that they would be sorry later? Or used a guilt-trip to make them feel lousy for not completing a commitment that they had started?

Probably, until an experience I had recently changed my mind about when is the right time to have a Bar or Bat Mitzvah.

In Hebrew, *Bar Mitzvah* means "son of the Commandments" and traditionally marked the transition, at age 13, from boyhood to manhood in Jewish personal and communal life. The Bar Mitzvah was the point at which a boy was able to be counted in the *minyan* (the quorum of 10 Jewish male adults necessary for certain prayers) and read from the Torah. Contemporary Judaism has expanded the rights and roles of women so that a girl who has reached her 12th birthday can now enjoy the same privileges as a 13- year-old-boy, including reading from the Torah and being part of the minyan.

But what happens to the many Jews who grow up without having a Bar/Bat Mitzvah at the age of 12 or 13? I found out when I was asked to work with a group of college students who expressed an interest in having one. Ranging between 19 and 23 years of age, each one had a story to share about why they hadn't done it earlier in their lives. Some, like Debbie's son Jason, just didn't want one when they were younger. Others came from interfaith families where it wasn't an option or from Jewish communities to which they didn't feel connected.

As they matured, each of my students developed a personal desire to learn more about Judaism in order to understand their relationship to their faith, God and Israel. They began our year of study together with commitment, enthusiasm and genuine intellectual curiosity that was palpable in our weekly hour and a half classes. As a teacher, I was honored to be a part of their spiritual journey toward Jewish adulthood. As a mother of a college student myself, I was rewarded by having this very intimate opportunity to learn about the struggles, fears, doubts and joys of college existence and offer my students a Jewish lens through which to view their lives.

We studied Jewish history, holidays, ethics, rituals and prayers while building a trusting and genuine spiritual community. We shared holidays, birthdays, exam anxiety and weight gain. I watched them struggle with questions of faith and heard them share their doubts, guilt and fears as they actively searched to find meaning in and from Judaism.

Our year of study culminated in a Shabbat morning service where each student read from the Torah and offered a *D'var Torah*, or personal interpretation or teaching, about something important that he or she had learned or grappled with during the year.

Anyone who had ever struggled with issues of faith, God or family was able to glean both wisdom and inspiration from my students that day. Individually and as a community of learners, they had engaged in the type of serious Jewish study that would now enable them to become responsible Jewish adults. And that, in a nutshell, is the crux of what it means to become a Bar or Bat Mitzvah.

At the end of the service, I offered my students the following words which I shared with Debbie in the hope that they might give her a different perspective about Jason's reluctance to have a Bar Mitzvah.

"Being Jewish is not like being in a race. You don't have to worry about getting to the finish line or keeping pace with other runners. There is no record or timekeeper, other than your innermost self, to mark your spiritual growth and progress.

"Being Jewish is about making the journey, about finding your own stride, about determining your own path. It is about taking that leap of faith and crossing through waters of doubt, discomfort and fear in order to better understand yourself, your family, your traditions, your history and your people. And it is in this way, when you are ready, that you will come to appreciate your uniqueness as an individual and your special destiny as a member of the Jewish people."

Bathing in the Waters of Paradise

The first time I saw a mikveh I had no idea what it was. My college roommate took me to a small building behind her synagogue that looked like a storage unit. We entered a dimly lit area where a small, green-tiled pool dominated the shabby room. It was hardly appealing, and I was shocked when she told me that Jewish women immersed themselves in it before they got married.

"My mother told me that the rain waters that fill it are like the waters of Eden," she whispered as we left.

The next time I encountered a mikveh was in reading *The Ritual Bath*, a mystery novel by Faye Kellerman. While the moving descriptions of the Orthodox women who went to the mikveh had a powerful hold on me, I never thought that I would go to one myself.

Several years later, I made a decision that was life-altering: I decided to leave my law practice and pursue my passion for Jewish learning. I wanted to do something special and spiritually significant to elevate my choice into something more than just a career change. That's when it hit me. I would begin my journey into Jewish learning by preparing myself in a very Jewish way: I would study the texts and go to the mikveh. To this day, it stands as one of the highlights in my quest to find ways to live a meaningful Jewish life.

Traditionally, mikveh is a thoroughly private experience so I feel somewhat uncomfortable writing about it. But I take some comfort in knowing that along with other traditional Jewish rituals that are being redefined today, there is renewed interest in mikveh observance as modern Jewish women discuss, explore and participate in mikveh for the first time.

The laws of family purity, or *taharat mishpacha*, date back to Biblical times. There are a lot of misconceptions and negative connotations about these laws, which have been viewed as primitive or demeaning to women by Jews who are not familiar with the reasons behind the laws. But mikveh lies at the heart of Jewish life because it offers us the opportunity to become spiritually pure and to perpetuate Jewish life and Jewish living.

Leviticus 18:19 and 20:18 prohibits marital relations during a woman's menstrual cycle and for seven "spotless" days thereafter. A woman goes to the mikveh to become spiritually pure, not physically clean, as those who misunderstand the ritual suggest. If we understand menstruation as a reflection of a woman's unique potential to create life, then we can appreciate a ritual that honors the renewal of a woman's capacity to conceive.

Mikveh attendance requires conscious, vigorous preparation including bathing, washing and combing the hair, cutting fingernails, and removing all jewelry, makeup or anything that is a barrier between a woman and the mikveh waters. It gives a woman the opportunity to luxuriate in being "squeaky clean" and offers a time to focus on the miracles of being a woman.

Traditionally, the mikveh was used by both men and women for various purposes including conversions, *kashering* utensils and purifying oneself after coming into contact with a ritually unclean person or item (*tamei* in Hebrew).

Today, Jewish women are reclaiming mikveh to celebrate important life-cycle events and provide meaningful rituals in times of loss, tragedy and sickness. Women also go to the mikveh to mark the onset of menopause, the end of a marriage, a trip to Israel and in my case, a change in careers.

Many community *mikvot* are open to all Jewish women before Rosh Hashanah and Yom Kippur for the purpose of spiritually preparing themselves for the year ahead. What a wonderful mitzvah to add to our lives as we embrace the New Year and the joys of being a Jewish woman.

The Jewish Sabbath: Time to Put My Octopus to Bed

I have a problem sleeping. To be more precise, I have a problem sleeping past six o'clock in the morning. No matter that it's the weekend or I've stayed up late the night before; when the sun rises, so do I.

This is not something I'm proud of—like a rigorous training schedule I endure in order to run a marathon someday. It is simply a childhood habit that I have been unable to break.

It all started in the spring of my tenth year when my father decided I was officially old enough to become a "full working member" of our family. For him this meant that I was the primary beneficiary of a 6:00 a.m. wake-up call that could be heard in the next county. For me it meant the end of any hope of watching cartoons and a list of chores that had to be done before noon.

The net result of this early morning ritual was twofold. First, it turned me into a morning person. You know the type: disgustingly cheerful and perky after having accomplished half a day's work before most people have even brushed their teeth. Second, it taught me Dad's Number One Life Lesson: To live is to work. (Not to be confused with Mom's Number One Life Lesson: To live is to worry.)

Don't get me wrong. Getting up early definitely had its advantages—like being the first one in our family to claim the prize in the Frosted Flakes box, or having grown-up conversations with my Dad about things like mortgages and snow blowers. Yet the afterglow of these small victories did not outweigh the long-term negative effect of equating rest with something I've earned only after all of my chores are done.

Over the years the fallacy of this way of thinking has become painfully clear, for the simple reason that getting all of my chores done is as probable as putting an octopus to bed. As soon as I have finished wrestling three arms into submission, two more emerge demanding my attention. Regardless of how many meals I cook, how much mail I open or how many hours I spend at the computer, there is always another phone call to return or one more column to write—all with my name on it!

I'm not alone in this struggle; I watch as my friends and co-workers juggle family, career and community life with barely enough time to breathe. On the never-ending treadmill of life's demands, we can't seem to find the 'off' button.

From the beginning of time, Jews have been commanded to differentiate between work and rest, between doing and being. We are taught that God created the world in six days and blessed the seventh day as holy because He rested from all that He had created. Shabbat, the Hebrew word for Sabbath, is a weekly holiday that teaches us what it means to stop, if only for a while.

The Jewish Sabbath begins on Friday night at sundown and lasts until Saturday evening. It has been called "a sanctuary in time," a holy framework that permits us to stop and reflect on how rich our lives can be when we relinquish control over the things we dominate, and that dominate us, during the week. It is meant to free us from the pressures and burdens of work, carpool and errands and enable us to renew ourselves through weekly relaxation, spiritual rest and renewal.

Shabbat is an invitation to enjoy time with family and friends, to share a good meal, to pray with our community, to finally finish the last chapter of the book we put down weeks ago for lack of time. It establishes a specific time each week during which we are entitled, even required, to pause and contemplate rather than to do and create.

Our sages taught that "More than Israel has kept the Shabbat, Shabbat has kept Israel." The meaning of this becomes clear when I see how I become a better mother, a more attentive wife, a more caring daughter, and ultimately a more engaged Jew, when I put the weekly demands of my work away in order to just "be."

Shabbat gives me an opportunity to put my octopus to bed. It helps me focus on what is most important in my life and teaches me the discipline of *not doing*. And while I know that there will still be clothes to wash and bills to pay when Shabbat is over, I always feel better for having let go, if only for a while.

About the Author

Amy Hirshberg Lederman is an award-winning, nationally syndicated columnist and author, Jewish educator, public speaker, and attorney. She practiced law for 14 years before pursuing her passion of Jewish education. She has served as the Assistant North American Director of the  Florence Melton Adult Mini-School and the Director of the Department of Jewish Education and Identity for the Jewish Federation of Southern Arizona. She currently teaches courses on Jewish spirituality, ethics, law and literature.

Amy received her Bachelor of Arts degree from Oberlin College, her Juris Doctor from the University of Arizona and her Master's Degree in Jewish Education from the Spertus College of Jewish Studies. In 1997-98, Amy moved with her family to Israel where she was part of an international group of Jewish educators who studied at Hebrew University.

Amy's presentations range from Jewish Federation,

synagogue and Hebrew Day School retreats to author book groups and seminars for Hadassah and the Anti-Defamation League. She has a nationally syndicated column featured in more than a dozen Jewish newspapers, has published stories in *Chicken Soup for the Jewish Soul, Chicken Soup for Every Mom's Soul* and is a contributor to the *Jewish World Review*. Her reputation as the Ethics Maven earned her a featured spot on "Too Jewish," a Jewish radio show aired weekly in the southwest. In 2005, Amy published her first book *To Life! Jewish Reflections on Everyday Living* (Aliyah Publishing LLC).

She is available to work with communities in areas of leadership development, community building/philanthropy, Jewish ethics, and family education. Current speaking topics include, but are not limited to:

- Finding the Leader Within: Jewish Models of Leadership
- Jewish Leadership: Making Your Time and Commitment Count!
- The Art of Jewish Giving: Making a Meaningful Gift
- My Grandmother's Candlesticks: Passing the Flame from One Generation to the Next
- Chicken Soup and Candlesticks: Creating Meaningful Jewish Rituals for Home and Family
- Honor Your Parents, Teach Your Children: Building Healthier Jewish Families
- *Lech Lecha*: The Jewish Search for Meaning and Purpose

- Ethical Wills: Creating a Legacy of Love and Values (writing workshop available)
- Putting God in your Briefcase: Finding Spirituality in the Workplace
- Being a Good Jew in a Complicated World
- Fascinating Jewish Trials that Changed History (Series or individual cases)

FOR MORE INFORMATION ABOUT HAVING AMY SPEAK IN YOUR COMMUNITY CONTACT HER AT:
www.amyhirshberglederman.com

About the Artist

Gail T. Roberts is more than the artist who created the painting on the cover of this book. She is one of my oldest and dearest friends and a spiritual companion who has introduced me to people, places and ideas that have changed my very being. I owe to her a lifetime  of gratitude for loving me in every stage of life and for knowing that a hippie doctor from Los Angeles would turn out to be my soul mate. I can not imagine my life without her.

The creation and publication of this book has been a wonderful journey and the thrill of collaborating with Gail on the artwork only increased the pleasure. I have provided information about Gail so that you may contact her if you would like to see more of her artwork.

This is what Gail Roberts says about her art:

"During my 30 years of artistic exploration, I have been a professional studio potter, painter, teacher, director of an art studio and a public artist. Each aspect of art offers new opportunities for me to learn and grow.

"In recent years, I have gone from working solo to expanding my business to include other artists as well as community volunteers. In my small studio in Tucson, Arizona, staff and volunteers gather to assist in my larger commissions and community art projects and to further explore their own artistic expression. Here we have constant collaboration—a joining together of creative energies, inspiring us to expand on that which is possible within and among us.

"This process of collaboration is an exciting aspect of the art I create and the work I do. Working in partnership with a lifelong friend, who has become a well-loved literary artist, is rich beyond words. Amy's clarity of vision made the process of designing her book cover almost wordless, opening up the channels for intuitions to surge forward. And it is this magic that best describes how the painting of the cover of *One God, Many Paths: Finding Meaning and Inspiration in Jewish Teachings* unfolded."

IF YOU WOULD LIKE TO CONTACT GAIL OR SEE MORE OF HER ART, PLEASE VISIT HER WEBSITE AT: www.gailtrobertsarts.com.